PROGRAM EVALUATION
IN GIFTED EDUCATION

ESSENTIAL READINGS IN GIFTED EDUCATION

SERIES EDITOR

SALLY M. REIS

Carolyn M. Callahan

EDITOR

PROGRAM EVALUATION IN GIFTED EDUCATION

A Joint Publication of Corwin Press and the National Association for Gifted Children

ESSENTIAL READINGS IN GIFTED EDUCATION
Sally M. Reis, SERIES EDITOR

CORWIN PRESS
A Sage Publications Company
Thousand Oaks, California

For information:

Corwin Press
A Sage Publications Company
2455 Teller Road
Thousand Oaks, California 91320
www.corwinpress.com

Sage Publications Ltd
1 Oliver's Yard
55 City Road
London EC1Y 1SP
United Kingdom

Sage Publications India Pvt. Ltd.
B-42, Panchsheel Enclave
Post Box 4109
New Delhi 110 017 India

Printed in the United States of America

Library of Congress Cataloging-in-Publication Data

A catalog record for this book is available from the Library of Congress.

ISBN 1-4129-0436-6

This book is printed on acid-free paper.

04 05 06 07 08 10 9 8 7 6 5 4 3 2 1

Acquisitions Editor:	Kylee Liegl
Editorial Assistant:	Jaime Cuvier
Production Editor:	Sanford Robinson
Typesetter:	C&M Digitals (P) Ltd.
Cover Designer:	Tracy E. Miller
NAGC Publications Coordinator:	Jane Clarenbach

Contents

About the Editors

Sally M. Reis is a professor and the department head of the Educational Psychology Department at the University of Connecticut where she also serves as principal investigator of the National Research Center on the Gifted and Talented. She was a teacher for 15 years, 11 of which were spent working with gifted students on the elementary, junior high, and high school levels. She has authored more than 130 articles, 9 books, 40 book chapters, and numerous monographs and technical reports.

Her research interests are related to special populations of gifted and talented students, including: students with learning disabilities, gifted females and diverse groups of talented students. She is also interested in extensions of the Schoolwide Enrichment Model for both gifted and talented students and as a way to expand offerings and provide general enrichment to identify talents and potentials in students who have not been previously identified as gifted.

She has traveled extensively conducting workshops and providing professional development for school districts on gifted education, enrichment programs, and talent development programs. She is co-author of *The Schoolwide Enrichment Model*, *The Secondary Triad Model*, *Dilemmas in Talent Development in the Middle Years*, and a book published in 1998 about women's talent development titled *Work Left Undone: Choices and Compromises of Talented Females*. Sally serves on several editorial boards, including the *Gifted Child Quarterly*, and is a past president of the National Association for Gifted Children.

Carolyn M. Callahan received her Ph.D. in the area of Educational Psychology with an emphasis in gifted education from the University of Connecticut. Since that time she has been on the faculty of the University of Virginia where she has developed the graduate program in gifted education, the Summer and Saturday Program for gifted students, and has been the director of the University of Virginia National Research Center on the Gifted and Talented for the past

12 years. She has done research across a broad range of topics in gifted education including the areas of the identification of gifted students, the evaluation of gifted programs, the development of performance assessments, and gifted program options. In collaboration with the other staff of the University of Virginia program, she has developed and delivered the highly successful annual Summer Institute on Academic Diversity for the past 5 years. Further, she was one of the editors of *Aiming for Excellence: Gifted Program Standards*, which is now widely used as the framework of criteria against which gifted programs are judged.

As part of her work outside the university, Dr. Callahan has worked with over 300 public school districts across nearly every state in the development of program designs, curriculum, and evaluations.

Finally, Dr. Callahan has received recognition as Outstanding Faculty Member in the Commonwealth of Virginia, Outstanding Professor of the Curry School of Education, Distinguished Higher Education Alumnae of the University of Connecticut, and was awarded the Distinguished Scholar Award from the National Association for Gifted Children. She is a past president of The Association for the Gifted and the National Association for Gifted Children. She also sits on the editorial boards of *Gifted Child Quarterly, Journal for the Education of the Gifted,* and *Roeper Review.*

Series Introduction

Sally M. Reis

The accomplishments of the last 50 years in the education of gifted students should not be underestimated: the field of education of the gifted and talented has emerged as strong and visible. In many states, a policy or position statement from the state board of education supports the education of the gifted and talented, and specific legislation generally recognizes the special needs of this group. Growth in our field has not been constant, however, and researchers and scholars have discussed the various high and low points of national interest and commitment to educating the gifted and talented (Gallagher, 1979; Renzulli, 1980; Tannenbaum, 1983). Gallagher described the struggle between support and apathy for special programs for gifted and talented students as having roots in historical tradition—the battle between an aristocratic elite and our concomitant belief in egalitarianism. Tannenbaum suggested the existence of two peak periods of interest in the gifted as the five years following *Sputnik* in 1957 and the last half of the decade of the 1970s, describing a valley of neglect between the peaks in which the public focused its attention on the disadvantaged and the handicapped. "The cyclical nature of interest in the gifted is probably unique in American education. No other special group of children has been alternately embraced and repelled with so much vigor by educators and laypersons alike" (Tannenbaum, 1983, p. 16). Many wonder if the cyclical nature to which Tannenbaum referred is not somewhat prophetic, as it appears that our field may be experiencing another downward spiral in interest as a result of current governmental initiatives and an increasing emphasis on testing and standardization of curriculum. Tannenbaum's description of a valley of neglect may describe current conditions. During the late 1980s, programming flourished during a peak of interest and a textbook on systems and models for gifted programs included 15 models for elementary and secondary programs (Renzulli, 1986). The Jacob Javits Gifted and Talented Students Education Act passed by Congress in 1988 resulted in the creation of the National Research Center on the Gifted and Talented, and dozens of model programs were added to the collective knowledge in the field in areas related to underrepresented populations and successful practices. In the 1990s, reduction or elimination of gifted programs occurred, as budget pressures exacerbated by the lingering recession in the late 1990s resulted in the reduction of services mandated by fewer than half of the states in our country.

Even during times in which more activity focused on the needs of gifted and talented students, concerns were still raised about the limited services provided to these students. In the second federal report on the status of education for our nation's most talented students entitled *National Excellence: A Case for Developing America's Talent* (Ross, 1993), "a quiet crisis" was described in the absence of attention paid to this population: "Despite sporadic attention over the years to the needs of bright students, most of them continue to spend time in school working well below their capabilities. The belief espoused in school reform that children from all economic and cultural backgrounds must reach their full potential has not been extended to America's most talented students. They are under-challenged and therefore underachieve" (p. 5). The report further indicates that our nation's gifted and talented students have a less rigorous curriculum, read fewer demanding books, and are less prepared for work or postsecondary education than the most talented students in many other industrialized countries. Talented children who come from economically disadvantaged homes or are members of minority groups are especially neglected, the report also indicates, and many of them will not realize their potential without some type of intervention.

In this anniversary series of volumes celebrating the evolution of our field, noted scholars introduce a collection of the most frequently cited articles from the premiere journal in our field, *Gifted Child Quarterly*. Each volume includes a collection of thoughtful, and in some cases, provocative articles that honor our past, acknowledge the challenges we face in the present, and provide hopeful guidance for the future as we seek the optimal educational experiences for all talented students. These influential articles, published after a rigorous peer review, were selected because they are frequently cited and considered seminal in our field. Considered in their entirety, the articles show that we have learned a great deal from the volume of work represented by this series. Our knowledge has expanded over several decades of work, and progress has been made toward reaching consensus about what is known. As several of the noted scholars who introduce separate areas explain in their introductions, this series helps us to understand that some questions have been answered, while others remain. While we still search for these answers, we are now better prepared to ask questions that continue and evolve. The seminal articles in this series help us to resolve some issues, while they highlight other questions that simply refuse to go away. Finally, the articles help us to identify new challenges that continue to emerge in our field. Carol Tomlinson suggests, for example, that the area of curriculum differentiation in the field of gifted education is, in her words, an issue born in the field of gifted education, and one that continues to experience rebirth.

Some of the earliest questions in our field have been answered and time has enabled those answers to be considered part of our common core of knowledge. For example, it is widely acknowledged that both school and home experiences can help to develop giftedness in persons with high potential and that a continuum of services in and out of school can provide the greatest likelihood that this development will occur. Debates over other "hot" issues such as grouping and acceleration that took place in the gifted education community 30 years ago are now largely unnecessary, as Linda Brody points out in her introduction to a series of articles in this area. General agreement seems to have been reached, for example, that grouping, enrichment and acceleration are all necessary to provide appropriate educational opportunities for gifted and talented learners. These healthy debates of the past helped to strengthen our field but visionary and reflective work remains to be done. In this series, section editors summarize what has been learned and raise provocative questions about the future. The questions alone are some of the most thoughtful in our field, providing enough research opportunities for scholars for the next decade. The brief introductions below provide some highlights about the series.

DEFINITIONS OF GIFTEDNESS (VOLUME 1)

In Volume 1, Robert Sternberg introduces us to seminal articles about definitions of giftedness and the types of talents and gifts exhibited by children and youth. The most widely used definitions of gifts and talents utilized by educators generally follow those proposed in federal reports. For example, the Marland Report (Marland, 1972) commissioned by the Congress included the first federal definition of giftedness, which was widely adopted or adapted by the states.

The selection of a definition of giftedness has been and continues to be the major policy decision made at state and local levels. It is interesting to note that policy decisions are often either unrelated or marginally related to actual procedures or to research findings about a definition of giftedness or identification of the gifted, a fact well documented by the many ineffective, incorrect, and downright ridiculous methods of identification used to find students who meet the criteria in the federal definition. This gap between policy and practice may be caused by many variables. Unfortunately, although the federal definition was written to be inclusive, it is, instead, rather vague, and problems caused by this definition have been recognized by experts in the field (Renzulli, 1978). In the most recent federal report on the status of gifted and talented programs entitled *National Excellence* (Ross, 1993), a newer federal definition is proposed based on new insights provided by neuroscience and cognitive psychology. Arguing that the term *gifted* connotes a mature power rather than a developing ability and, therefore, is antithetic to recent research findings about children, the new definition "reflects today's knowledge and thinking" (p. 26) by emphasizing talent development, stating that gifted and talented children are children and youth with outstanding talent performance or show the potential for performing at remarkably high levels of accomplishment when compared with others of their age, experience, or environment. These children and youth exhibit high performance capability in intellectual, creative, and/or artistic areas, possess an unusual leadership capacity, or excel in specific academic fields. They require services or activities not ordinarily provided by the schools. Outstanding talents are present in children and youth from all cultural groups, across all economic strata, and in all areas of human endeavor. (p. 26)

Fair identification systems use a variety of multiple assessment measures that respect diversity, accommodate students who develop at different rates, and identify potential as well as demonstrated talent. In the introduction to the volume, Sternberg admits, that just as people have bad habits, so do academic fields, explaining, "a bad habit of much of the gifted field is to do research on giftedness, or worse, identify children as gifted or not gifted, without having a clear conception of what it means to be gifted." Sternberg summarizes major themes from the seminal articles about definitions by asking key questions about the nature of giftedness and talent, the ways in which we should study giftedness, whether we should expand conventional notions of giftedness, and if so, how that can be accomplished; whether differences exist between giftedness and talent; the validity of available assessments; and perhaps most importantly, how do we and can we develop giftedness and talent. Sternberg succinctly summarizes points of broad agreement from the many scholars who have contributed to this section, concluding that giftedness involves more than just high IQ, that it has noncognitive and cognitive components, that the environment is crucial in terms of whether potentials for gifted performance will be realized, and that giftedness is not a single thing. He further cautions that the ways we conceptualize giftedness greatly influences who will have opportunities to develop their gifts and reminds readers of our responsibilities as educators. He also asks one of the most critical questions in our field: whether gifted and talented individuals will use their knowledge to benefit or harm our world.

IDENTIFICATION OF HIGH-ABILITY STUDENTS (VOLUME 2)

In Volume 2, Joseph Renzulli introduces what is perhaps the most critical question still facing practitioners and researchers in our field, that is how, when, and why should we identify gifted and talented students. Renzulli believes that conceptions of giftedness exist along a continuum ranging from a very conservative or restricted view of giftedness to a more flexible or multidimensional approach. What many seem not to understand is that the first step in identification should always be to ask: identification for what? For what type of program or experience is the youngster being identified? If, for example, an arts program is being developed for talented artists, the resulting identification system must be structured to identify youngsters with either demonstrated or potential talent in art.

Renzulli's introductory chapter summarizes seminal articles about identification, and summarizes emerging consensus. For example, most suggest, that while intelligence tests and other cognitive ability tests provide one very important form of information about one dimension of a young person's potential, mainly in the areas of verbal and analytic skills, they do not tell us all that we need to know about who should be identified. These authors do not argue that cognitive ability tests should be dropped from the identification process. Rather, most believe that (a) other indicators of potential should be used for identification, (b) these indicators should be given equal consideration when it comes to making final decisions about which students will be candidates for special services, and (c) in the final analysis, it is the thoughtful judgment of knowledgeable professionals rather than instruments and cutoff scores that should guide selection decisions.

Another issue addressed by the authors of the seminal articles about identification is what has been referred to as the distinction between (a) convergent and divergent thinking (Guilford, 1967; Torrance, 1984), (b) entrenchment and non-entrenchment (Sternberg, 1982), and (c) schoolhouse giftedness versus creative/productive giftedness (Renzulli, 1982; Renzulli & Delcourt, 1986). It is easier to identify schoolhouse giftedness than it is to identify students with the potential for creative productive giftedness. Renzulli believes that progress has been made in the identification of gifted students, especially during the past quarter century, and that new approaches address the equity issue, policies, and practices that respect new theories about human potential and conceptions of giftedness. He also believes, however, that continuous commitment to research-based identification practices is still needed, for "it is important to keep in mind that some of the characteristics that have led to the recognition of history's most gifted contributors are not always as measurable as others. We need to continue our search for those elusive things that are left over after everything explainable has been explained, to realize that giftedness is culturally and contextually imbedded in all human activity, and most of all, to value the value of even those things that we cannot yet explain."

ACCELERATION AND GROUPING, CURRICULUM, AND CURRICULUM DIFFERENTIATION (VOLUMES 3, 4, 5)

Three volumes in this series address curricular and grouping issues in gifted programs, and it is in this area, perhaps, that some of the most promising practices have been implemented for gifted and talented students. Grouping and curriculum interact with each other, as various forms of grouping patterns have enabled students to work on advanced curricular opportunities with other talented students. And, as is commonly known now about instructional and ability grouping, it is not the way students are grouped that matters most, but rather, it is what happens within the groups that makes the most difference.

In too many school settings, little differentiation of curriculum and instruction for gifted students is provided during the school day, and minimal opportunities are offered. Occasionally, after-school enrichment programs or Saturday programs offered by museums, science centers, or local universities take the place of comprehensive school programs, and too many academically talented students attend school in classrooms across the country in which they are bored, unmotivated, and unchallenged. Acceleration, once a frequently used educational practice in our country, is often dismissed by teachers and administrators as an inappropriate practice for a variety of reasons, including scheduling problems, concerns about the social effects of grade skipping, and others. Various forms of acceleration, including enabling precocious students to enter kindergarten or first grade early, grade skipping, and early entrance to college are not commonly used by most school districts.

Unfortunately, major alternative grouping strategies involve the reorganization of school structures, and these have been too slow in coming, perhaps due to the difficulty of making major educational changes, because of scheduling, finances, and other issues that have caused schools to substantially delay major change patterns. Because of this delay, gifted students too often fail to receive classroom instruction based on their unique needs that place them far ahead of their chronological peers in basic skills and verbal abilities and enable them to learn much more rapidly and tackle much more complex materials than their peers. Our most able students need appropriately paced, rich and challenging instruction, and curriculum that varies significantly from what is being taught in regular classrooms across America. Too often, academically talented students are "left behind" in school.

Linda Brody introduces the question of how to group students optimally for instructional purposes and pays particular concern to the degree to which the typical age-in-grade instructional program can meet the needs of gifted students—those students with advanced cognitive abilities and achievement that may already have mastered the curriculum designed for their age peers. The articles about grouping emphasize the importance of responding to the learning needs of individual students with curricular flexibility, the need for educators to be flexible when assigning students to instructional groups, and the need to modify those groups when necessary. Brody's introduction points out that the debate about grouping gifted and talented learners together was one area that brought the field together, as every researcher in the field supports some type of grouping option, and few would disagree with the need to use grouping and accelerated learning as tools that allow us to differentiate content for students with different learning needs. When utilized as a way to offer a more advanced educational program to students with advanced cognitive abilities and achievement levels, these practices can help achieve the goal of an appropriate education for all students.

Joyce VanTassel-Baska introduces the seminal articles in curriculum, by explaining that they represent several big ideas that emphasize the values and relevant factors of a curriculum for the gifted, the technology of curriculum development, aspects of differentiation of a curriculum for the gifted within core subject areas and without, and the research-based efficacy of such curriculum and related instructional pedagogy in use. She also reminds readers of Harry Passow's concerns about curriculum balance, suggesting that an imbalance exists, as little evidence suggests that the affective development of gifted students is occurring through special curricula for the gifted. Moreover, interdisciplinary efforts at curriculum frequently exclude the arts and foreign language. Only through acknowledging and applying curriculum balance in these areas are we likely to be producing the type of humane individual Passow envisioned. To achieve balance, VanTassel-Baska recommends a full set of curriculum options across domains, as well as the need to nurture the social-emotional needs of diverse gifted and talented learners.

Carol Tomlinson introduces the critical area of differentiation in the field of gifted education that has only emerged in the last 13 years. She believes the diverse nature of the articles and their relatively recent publication suggests that this area is indeed, in her words, "an issue born in the field of gifted education, and one that continues to experience rebirth." She suggests that one helpful way of thinking about the articles in this volume is that their approach varies, as some approach the topic of differentiation of curriculum with a greater emphasis on the distinctive mission of gifted education. Others look at differentiation with a greater emphasis on the goals, issues, and missions shared between general education and gifted education. Drawing from an analogy with anthropology, Tomlinson suggests that "splitters" in that field focus on differences among cultures while "lumpers" have a greater interest in what cultures share in common. Splitters ask the question of what happens for high-ability students in mixed-ability settings, while lumpers question what common issues and solutions exist for multiple populations in mixed-ability settings.

Tomlinson suggests that the most compelling feature of the collection of articles in this section—and certainly its key unifying feature—is the linkage between the two areas of educational practice in attempting to address an issue likely to be seminal to the success of both over the coming quarter century and beyond, and this collection may serve as a catalyst for next steps in those directions for the field of gifted education as it continues collaboration with general education and other educational specialties while simultaneously addressing those missions uniquely its own.

UNDERREPRESENTED AND TWICE-EXCEPTIONAL POPULATIONS AND SOCIAL AND EMOTIONAL ISSUES (VOLUMES 6, 7, 8)

The majority of young people participating in gifted and talented programs across the country continue to represent the majority culture in our society. Few doubts exist regarding the reasons that economically disadvantaged, twice-exceptional, and culturally diverse students are underrepresented in gifted programs. One reason may be the ineffective and inappropriate identification and selection procedures used for the identification of these young people that limits referrals and nominations and eventual placement. Research summarized in this series indicates that groups that have been traditionally underrepresented in gifted programs could be better served if some of the following elements are considered: new constructs of giftedness, attention to cultural and contextual variability, the use of more varied and authentic assessments, performance-based identification, and identification opportunities through rich and varied learning opportunities.

Alexinia Baldwin discusses the lower participation of culturally diverse and underserved populations in programs for the gifted as a major concern that has forged dialogues and discussion in *Gifted Child Quarterly* over the past five decades. She classifies these concerns in three major themes: *identification/selection*, *programming*, and *staff assignment and development*. Calling the first theme **Identification/Selection**, she indicates that it has always been the Achilles' heel of educators' efforts to ensure that giftedness can be expressed in many ways through broad identification techniques. Citing favorable early work by Renzulli and Hartman (1971) and Baldwin (1977) that expanded options for identification, Baldwin cautions that much remains to be done. The second theme, **Programming**, recognizes the abilities of students who are culturally diverse but often forces them to exist in programs designed "for one size fits all." Her third theme relates to **Staffing and Research**, as she voices concerns about the diversity of teachers in these programs as well as the attitudes or mindsets of researchers who develop theories and conduct the research that addresses these concerns.

Susan Baum traces the historical roots of gifted and talented individuals with special needs, summarizing Terman's early work that suggested the gifted were healthier, more popular, and better adjusted than their less able peers. More importantly, gifted individuals were regarded as those who could perform at high levels in all areas with little or no support. Baum suggests that acceptance of these stereotypical characteristics diminished the possibility that there could be special populations of gifted students with special needs. Baum believes that the seminal articles in this collection address one or more of the critical issues that face gifted students at risk and suggest strategies for overcoming the barriers that prevent them from realizing their promise. The articles focus on three populations of students: twice-exceptional students—gifted students who are at risk for poor development due to difficulties in learning and attention;

gifted students who face gender issues that inhibit their ability to achieve or develop socially and emotionally, and students who are economically disadvantaged and at risk for dropping out of school. Baum summarizes research indicating that each of these groups of youngsters is affected by one or more barriers to development, and the most poignant of these barriers are identification strategies, lack of awareness of consequences of co-morbidity, deficit thinking in program design, and lack of appropriate social and emotional support. She ends her introduction with a series of thoughtful questions focusing on future directions in this critical area.

Sidney Moon introduces the seminal articles on the social and emotional development of and counseling for gifted children by acknowledging the contributions of the National Association for Gifted Children's task forces that have examined social/emotional issues. The first task force, formed in 2000 and called the Social and Emotional Issues Task Force, completed its work in 2002 by publishing an edited book, *The Social and Emotional Development of Gifted Children: What Do We Know?* This volume provides an extensive review of the literature on the social and emotional development of gifted children (Neihart, Reis, Robinson, & Moon, 2002). Moon believes that the seminal studies in the area of the social and emotional development and counseling illustrate both the strengths and the weaknesses of the current literature on social and emotional issues in the field of gifted education. These articles bring increased attention to the affective needs of special populations of gifted students, such as underachievers, who are at risk for failure to achieve their potential, but also point to the need for more empirical studies on "what works" with these students, both in terms of preventative strategies and more intensive interventions. She acknowledges that although good counseling models have been developed, they need to be rigorously evaluated to determine their effectiveness under disparate conditions, and calls for additional research on the affective and counseling interventions with specific subtypes of gifted students such as Asian Americans, African Americans, and twice-exceptional students. Moon also strongly encourages researchers in the field of gifted education to collaborate with researchers from affective fields such as personal and social psychology, counseling psychology, family therapy, and psychiatry to learn to intervene most effectively with gifted individuals with problems and to learn better how to help all gifted persons achieve optimal social, emotional, and personal development.

ARTISTICALLY AND CREATIVELY TALENTED STUDENTS (VOLUMES 9, 10)

Enid Zimmerman introduces the volume on talent development in the visual and performing arts with a summary of articles about students who are talented in music, dance, visual arts, and spatial, kinesthetic, and expressive areas. Major themes that appear in the articles include perceptions by parents, students, and teachers that often focus on concerns related to nature versus nurture in arts talent development; research about the crystallizing experiences of artistically talented students; collaboration between school and community members about identification of talented art students from diverse backgrounds; and leadership issues related to empowering teachers of talented arts students. They all are concerned to some extent with teacher, parent, and student views about educating artistically talented students. Included also are discussions about identification of talented students from urban, suburban, and rural environments. Zimmerman believes that in this particular area, a critical need exists for research about the impact of educational opportunities, educational settings, and the role of art teachers on the development of artistically talented students. The impact of the standards and testing movement and its relationship to the education of talented students in the visual and performing arts is an area greatly in need of investigation. Research also is needed about students' backgrounds, personalities, gender orientations, skill development, and cognitive and affective abilities as well as cross-cultural contexts and the impact of global and popular culture on the education of artistically talented students. The compelling case study with which she introduces this volume sets the stage for the need for this research.

Donald Treffinger introduces reflections on articles about creativity by discussing the following five core themes that express the collective efforts of researchers to grasp common conceptual and theoretical challenges associated with creativity. The themes include **Definitions** (how we define giftedness, talent, or creativity), **Characteristics** (the indicators of giftedness and creativity in people), **Justification** (Why is creativity important in education?), **Assessment** of creativity, and the ways we **Nurture** creativity. Treffinger also discusses the expansion of knowledge, the changes that have occurred, the search for answers, and the questions that still remain. In the early years of interest of creativity research, Treffinger believed that considerable discussion existed about whether it was possible to foster creativity through training or instruction. He reports that over the last 50 years, educators have learned that deliberate efforts to nurture creativity are possible (e.g., Torrance, 1987), and further extends this line of inquiry by asking the key question, "What works best, for whom, and under what conditions?" Treffinger summarizes the challenges faced by educators who try to nurture the development of creativity through effective teaching and to ask which experiences will have the greatest impact, as these will help to determine our ongoing lines of research, development, and training initiatives.

EVALUATION AND PUBLIC POLICY (VOLUMES 11, 12)

Carolyn Callahan introduces the seminal articles on evaluation and suggests that this important component neglected by experts in the field of gifted education for at least the last three decades can be a plea for important work by both evaluators and practitioners. She divides the seminal literature on evaluation, and in particular the literature on the evaluation of gifted programs into four categories, those which (a) provide theory and/or practical guidelines, (b) describe or report on specific program evaluations, (c) provide stimuli for the discussion of issues surrounding the evaluation process, and (d) suggest new research on the evaluation process. Callahan concludes with a challenge indicating work to be done and the opportunity for experts to make valuable contributions to increased effectiveness and efficiency of programs for the gifted.

James Gallagher provides a call-to-arms in the seminal articles he introduces on public policy by raising some of the most challenging questions in the field. Gallagher suggests that as a field, we need to come to some consensus about stronger interventions and consider how we react to accusations of elitism. He believes that our field could be doing a great deal more with additional targeted resources supporting the general education teacher and the development of specialists in gifted education, and summarizes that our failure to fight in the public arena for scarce resources may raise again the question posed two decades ago by Renzulli (1980), looking toward 1990: "Will the gifted child movement be alive and well in 2010?"

CONCLUSION

What can we learn from an examination of our field and the seminal articles that have emerged over the last few decades? First, we must **respect the past** by acknowledging the times in which articles were written and the shoulders of those persons upon whom we stand as we continue to create and develop our field. An old proverb tells us that when we drink from the well, we must remember to acknowledge those who dug the well, and in our field the early articles represent the seeds that grew our field. Next, we must **celebrate the present** and the exciting work and new directions in our field and the knowledge that is now accepted as a common core. Last, we must **embrace the future** by understanding that there is no finished product when it comes to research on gifted and talented children and how we are best able to meet their unique needs. Opportunities abound in the work reported in this series, but many questions remain. A few things seem clear. Action in the future should be based on both qualitative and quantitative research as well as longitudinal studies, and what we have completed only scratches the surface regarding the many variables and issues that still need to be explored. Research is needed that suggests positive changes that will lead to more inclusive programs that recognize the talents and gifts of diverse students in our country. When this occurs, future teachers and researchers in gifted education will find answers that can be embraced by educators, communities, and families, and the needs of all talented and gifted students will be more effectively met in their classrooms by teachers who have been trained to develop their students' gifts and talents.

We also need to consider carefully how we work with the field of education in general. As technology emerges and improves, new opportunities will become available to us. Soon, all students should be able to have their curricular needs preassessed before they begin any new curriculum unit. Soon, the issue of keeping students on grade-level material when they are many grades ahead should disappear as technology enables us to pinpoint students' strengths. Will chronological grades be eliminated? The choices we have when technology enables us to learn better what students already know presents exciting scenarios for the future, and it is imperative that we advocate carefully for multiple opportunities for these students, based on their strengths and interests, as well as a challenging core curriculum. Parents, educators, and professionals who care about these special populations need to become politically active to draw attention to the unique needs of these students, and researchers need to conduct the experimental studies that can prove the efficacy of providing talent development options as well as opportunities for healthy social and emotional growth.

For any field to continue to be vibrant and to grow, new voices must be heard, and new players sought. A great opportunity is available in our field; for as we continue to advocate for gifted and talented students, we can also play important roles in the changing educational reform movement. We can continue to work to achieve more challenging opportunities for all students while we fight to maintain gifted, talented, and enrichment programs. We can continue our advocacy for differentiation through acceleration, individual curriculum opportunities, and a continuum of advanced curriculum and personal support opportunities. The questions answered and those raised in this volume of seminal articles can help us to move forward as a field. We hope those who read the series will join us in this exciting journey.

REFERENCES

Baldwin, A.Y. (1977). Tests do underpredict: A case study. *Phi Delta Kappan, 58,* 620-621.

Gallagher, J. J. (1979). Issues in education for the gifted. In A. H. Passow (Ed.), *The gifted and the talented: Their education and development* (pp. 28-44). Chicago: University of Chicago Press.

Guilford, J. E. (1967). *The nature of human intelligence.* New York: McGraw-Hill.

Marland, S. P., Jr. (1972). *Education of the gifted and talented: Vol. 1. Report to the Congress of the United States by the U.S. Commissioner of Education.* Washington, DC: U.S. Government Printing Office.

Neihart, M., Reis, S., Robinson, N., & Moon, S. M. (Eds.). (2002). *The social and emotional development of gifted children: What do we know?* Waco, TX: Prufrock.

Renzulli, J. S. (1978). What makes giftedness? Reexamining a definition. *Phi Delta Kappan, 60*(5), 180-184.

Renzulli, J. S. (1980). Will the gifted child movement be alive and well in 1990? *Gifted Child Quarterly, 24*(1), 3-9. **[See Vol. 12.]**

Renzulli, J. (1982). Dear Mr. and Mrs. Copernicus: We regret to inform you . . . *Gifted Child Quarterly, 26*(1), 11-14. **[See Vol. 2.]**

Renzulli, J. S. (Ed.). (1986). *Systems and models for developing programs for the gifted and talented.* Mansfield Center, CT: Creative Learning Press.

Renzulli, J. S., & Delcourt, M. A. B. (1986). The legacy and logic of research on the identification of gifted persons. *Gifted Child Quarterly, 30*(1), 20-23. **[See Vol. 2.]**

Renzulli J., & Hartman, R. (1971). Scale for rating behavioral characteristics of superior students. *Exceptional Children, 38,* 243-248.

Ross, P. (1993). *National excellence: A case for developing America's talent.* Washington, DC: U.S. Department of Education, Government Printing Office.

Sternberg, R. J. (1982). Nonentrenchment in the assessment of intellectual giftedness. *Gifted Child Quarterly, 26*(2), 63-67. **[See Vol. 2.]**

Tannenbaum, A. J. (1983). *Gifted children: Psychological and educational perspectives.* New York: Macmillan.

Torrance, E. P. (1984). The role of creativity in identification of the gifted and talented. *Gifted Child Quarterly, 28*(4), 153-156. **[See Vols. 2 and 10.]**

Torrance, E. P. (1987). Recent trends in teaching children and adults to think creatively. In S. G. Isaksen (Ed.), *Frontiers of creativity research: Beyond the basics* (pp. 204-215). Buffalo, NY: Bearly Limited.

Introduction to Program Evaluation in Gifted Education

Carolyn M. Callahan

University of Virginia

Program evaluation has been considered an important, but neglected, component by experts in the field of gifted education for at least the last three decades (Gallagher, 1979; Renzulli & Ward, 1969), but yet, the guidance given to the field about this essential area has been limited. *Gifted Child Quarterly* has been one vehicle used to provide important direction to evaluators and practitioners.

CATEGORIES OF EVALUATION

The literature on evaluation, and in particular the literature on the evaluation of gifted programs, may be divided into four categories. Included in the first of those categories are the manuscripts that provide theory and/or practical guidelines. These guidelines sometimes include particular suggestions for the evaluation of gifted programs in general or for the evaluation of specific components of a program such as evaluation of staff development and sometimes provide examples of instrumentation and/or suggestions for instrument development. These articles are represented in this volume by Callahan (1986), Carter and Hamilton (1985), Kulieke (1986), Lundsteen (1987), and Reis and Renzulli (1991). The second category of evaluation articles describes or reports on specific program evaluations. Such *Gifted Child Quarterly (GCQ)* articles as the VanTassel-Baska, Willis, and Meyer (1989) article summarize evaluations of the effectiveness of particular programs such as a self-contained program for gifted. The report by Avery, VanTassel-Baska, and O'Neill (1997) describes the evaluation of a suburban gifted program using multiple models, and Landrum (2001) documents the evaluation of a catalyst program using a consultation/collaboration approach to providing services for gifted students. The third category of program evaluation articles provides stimuli for the discussion of issues surrounding the evaluation process. For example, in this collection authors from outside the field of gifted education have published provocative ideas in *GCQ* that stimulate our thinking about alternatives to the evaluation of student performance. Baker and Schacter (1996) and Wiggins (1996) offer new ideas for the assessment of gifted students using expert performance as the basis for setting standards. The last category of evaluation articles, research on the evaluation process, is sadly missing from *Gifted Child Quarterly* and nearly absent from the literature on gifted program evaluation. Callahan, Tomlinson, Hunsaker, Bland, and Moon (1995) have conducted research on the factors that increase the likelihood that recommendations from program evaluations will be implemented. Hunsaker and Callahan (1993) examined the degree to which current evaluation practices in the field of gifted education utilized the multiple methodologies, sources, analysis techniques, and reporting formats recommended in the *Standards for the Evaluation of Educational Programs, Projects and Materials* (Joint Committee on Standards for Educational Evaluation, 1981). But these publications represent nearly the entire body of research on evaluation practice.

The articles that represent these four categories from *GCQ* in this volume have offered important guidance to the field because they raise significant issues. But the glaring omissions within each category and across categories suggest our work is not done.

Category I: Guidelines for Evaluating Programs and Products

A set of common and useful principles cut across the articles in this category, with individual authors each offering unique variations on the themes. The importance of formative is stressed by Carter and Hamilton (1985) based on assumptions about the importance of gifted programming, but Callahan stresses the importance of addressing all questions of audiences served by the evaluation including summative evaluation questions. Commonalities or agreed upon principles of program evaluation include: carefully planning to ensure that the evaluation addresses the concerns of critical players in the program; narrowing the evaluation questions to those of most critical importance; ensuring that data collection is systematic; recognizing and acting on the importance of creating a collaborative relationship between evaluator and client; ensuring that student product outcomes be considered as one focus of the evaluation plan; ensuring that data collection is systematic, appropriate to the question posed, and carefully weighed; and finally, that communication is clear and timely (Callahan, 1986; Carter & Hamilton, 1985).

One of the particular suggestions that deserves attention is that evaluations be designed to address not just "easy to answer" evaluation questions with easy to construct instruments, but that evaluations address the most important questions for good decision making, and that evaluation data collection use the most direct and valid tools. Using staff development as her example, Kulieke (1986) notes that while questionnaires will provide data on teachers' perceptions of their needs and competencies, she also stresses the importance of direct observation in ascertaining the actual teaching behaviors and the quality of implementation of teaching strategies appropriate for gifted learners.

Kulieke has also made a significant contribution by providing an example of the use of the evaluation process as a valuable tool in needs assessment. While all evaluators talk of the use of evaluation data in the development of recommendations for program improvement, her discussion of needs assessment is a concrete example of the way an evaluation process can directly inform program decisions. Her outline of the ways in which evaluation data collected about particular types of inservice programs illustrates the range of purposes that evaluation can serve, as is outlined by Callahan and Caldwell (1986, 1995). Kulieke's approach also exemplifies ways in which evaluation can provide information on the degree to which the program design meets identified needs of the target audience, the degree to which a program is implemented as designed, and the degree to which behaviors are changed or learning occurs as a result of program implementation.

Callahan (1986) and Carter and Hamilton (1985) both stress the importance of including key decision makers in the selection of foci for an evaluation. However, Carter and Hamilton define the decision makers as the administrators of the program and only suggest going beyond that group in the case where administrators do not have clear goals for the evaluation, while Callahan expands the initial concept of decision makers to include both internal audiences and external audiences who have a stake in the program's effectiveness.

Another commonality of the Callahan (1986) and Carter and Hamilton (1985) approaches is the identification of essential components of gifted programs that should be considered as targets of the evaluation process. Both of these lists of essential components resemble the Key Features of Program for the Gifted that were identified by Renzulli (1975), but should now be updated to reflect the standards for excellence in gifted programs that have been elucidated by the National Association for Gifted Children to include: Program Design, Program Administration and Management, Curriculum and Instruction, Student Identification, Professional Development, Social and Emotional Guidance ad Counseling, and Program Evaluation (Landrum, Callahan, & Shaklee, 2001).

As the process of selecting the more narrow questions within each of these categories evolves, the literature suggests questions of concern to internal and external audiences, questions relating to the central functioning of the program, questions that history suggests represent potential problems that may inhibit good program functioning, and questions where information is needed soon for decision making should take priority (Callahan, 1986).

These authors also present the recurrent theme of the importance of selecting or creating reliable and valid instruments and strategies for collecting data for the decision-making processes of evaluation—whether the evaluation question focuses on process or student outcomes. Carter and Hamilton (1985) note the importance of considering the type of evaluation question and matching both the strategy and the particular data collection instrument selected to the evaluation questions. Like Wiggins (1996), Callahan (1986) and Reis and Renzulli (1991) point out the weaknesses inherent in using only paper-and-pencil, standardized tests to assess student outcomes. But, as this collection illustrates so vividly, little has been done to expand the available collection of alternative instruments that have been subjected to the rigors of psychometric examination. Kulieke (1986) offers an instrument of classroom observation based on the *Martinson-Weiner Rating Scale of Behaviors in Teachers of the Gifted* (Martinson, 1976), but does not provide reliability or validity data. The only alternative instrument offered with the expected, adequate psychometric properties is the *Student Product Assessment Form* (SPAF) (Reis & Renzulli, 1991). The review of the related literature in this article illustrates the field's lack of validated instruments to assess students' creative products, but provides good news about one instrument with excellent statistical properties that could be widely used.

Category II: Descriptions of Specific Program Evaluations

The evaluation summaries of Avery, VanTassel-Baska, and O'Neill (1997), Landrum (2001), and VanTassel-Baska, Willis, and Meyer (1989) are valuable in illustrating how the general principles presented in the articles discussed in the first category might be applied, but they also illustrate the continued lack of development of instruments to assess student outcome goals. In presenting the results of an evaluation of a local district program, Avery, VanTassel-Baska, and O'Neill (1997) illustrate the ways in which the questions of classroom observations may be used to determine whether or not the curriculum and instructional strategies are differentiated appropriately. This evaluation also provides guidance in outlining the ways in which reporting and communicating results through multiple vehicles enhances utilization of results.

However, as Avery, VanTassel-Baska, and O'Neill (1997) point out, "the traditional linch [sic] pin of student performance" is not addressed in this report, (p. 124) nor is it addressed in the report of Landrum. However, Landrum (2001) has provided a creative example of using alternative data sources as a means of judging the effectiveness of implementing a new program model and using subjects as their own control over a period of time. By collecting data on: changes in use of classroom instructional strategies; the frequency of opportunity for gifted students to engage in activities that might be characterized as more rigorous; and standardized test performance, Landrum confirmed the effects of the implementation of a consultation model on classroom behaviors of teachers.

The evaluation of the full-time, self-contained classroom (VanTassel-Baska, Willis, & Meyer, 1989) illustrates one strategy for finding a comparison group to use as a basis for attributing the changes in student test scores to the program intervention. One additional important consideration that is suggested by the analysis in this article is the need to present and discuss effect sizes. With such large samples we may find significant, but meaningful effects.

But these evaluations also point to the difficulty in establishing adequate comparison groups and the difficulty in identifying adequate instruments for measuring student outcome variables.

Category III: Issues in Evaluation

A careful presentation of arguments for and against setting expert performance as the standard in assessing student performance in programs for the gifted is provided by Baker and Schacter (1996) and Wiggins (1996). Baker and Schacter also offer the possibility of using performances of teachers with content expertise to establish the levels of expertise we would set as goals for student achievement. A third possibility they offer is to use the performances of identified gifted students. Their discussion of these possibilities raises issues of developmentally appropriate considerations, but importantly, suggests areas of potentially valuable research in the area of evaluation of student outcomes. Wiggins acknowledges the potential resistance to setting standards using superlative performance as the goal, but argues, "faculties should always calibrate their local standards to such exemplars, anchoring the highest point in their scoring system with such examples of excellent performance. It is the only way for teachers as well as students to have valid, compelling, stable targets at which to aim" (p. 66). He further cautions against the overemphasis on process, form, and content in student products while stressing the importance of evaluating the effect of products if we wish to preserve the development of creativity—the degree to which the products "persuade an audience, satisfy a client request, or solve a problem" (p. 67). His discussion of expectations versus standards is a compelling argument for continued exploration and debate about the use of this approach.

DEFICITS IN OUR LITERATURE BASE IN EVALUATION

One of the characteristics of a collection of articles from journal such as *GCQ*, or any other research-oriented journal, is that the manuscripts are reviewed using stringent criteria for traditional experimental design (although more recently, the qualitative paradigm has received increasing attention). Evaluations are not research studies with expectations of strictly controlled experimental and control groups, and they are not designed with expectations for generalizability to other settings or with the expectation of expanding the general knowledge base. Because evaluations do not and should not/cannot be expected to adhere to these rigid criteria, they are not likely to be published. Further, most evaluations are carried out with expectations on the part of the program and school district that the information gathered has the purpose of informing the program only of the strengths, weaknesses, and accomplishments of a particular school district's efforts in meeting the needs of the gifted. Hence, the practical examples of good evaluation are limited in the research base. Only authors who are able to gain the permission of the districts with which they work to "expose" the findings are able to translate the particular evaluation report into a publishable manuscript. And only those authors who are able to frame the evaluation study as exemplars of evaluation or who have been fortunate enough to be able to create some semblance of a comparison group have been successful in bringing the knowledge learned from evaluation studies to the public domain.

Examples of Lessons Learned

The limitations discussed above have deprived our field of important information that could be used to guide others in the formulation of plans for the oft-neglected, but critical, aspect of program planning and revision. Evaluators who are actively engaged in the important process of gathering data on program process and products should be giving consideration to using the lessons that they learn through the evaluation process to inform others who either execute evaluation themselves or seek to engage outside, independent evaluators. Particularly, there is a need to explicate ways in which the difficult question of program impact can be addressed by careful, creative, and systematic data collection. Informing others of the existence of useful assessment tools and providing data on the reliability and validity of new, innovative assessment tools as Reis and Renzulli (1991) have done.

Longitudinal Evaluation

One of the most neglected aspects of the evaluation of gifted programs has been longitudinal or long-term impact assessment. The evaluation studies in this compendium (Avery, VanTassel-Baska, & O'Neill, 1997; Landrum, 2001; VanTassel-Baska, Willis, & Meyer, 1989) report on student outcomes that represent the impact across one- to two-year assessment periods. The literature fails to carefully track or provide a model for the evaluation of the impact of school programs across the span of the child's career in a gifted program—particularly as the program spans the elementary, middle, and high school years. Hertzog (2003) lamented the lack of evaluation data that provides program decision-makers with evidence of lasting or cumulative effects of programming strategies or curricular modifications. Like longitudinal research, longitudinal evaluation studies require unique planning and investments of resources—both time and energy—that go beyond the ordinary or evaluations that are in response to "crises" in the gifted program. Gifted program evaluation that is implemented "at the moment" is hampered in the assessment of long-term effects by several factors. First, without anticipatory planning, student databases are not created to ensure that tracking of students is possible, that careful plans are designed and executed to ensure appropriate assessment intervals with careful selection or creation of outcome measures, that students who leave the program or school district are either monitored or even noted, etc.

Longitudinal evaluation, as all evaluation, requires that school personnel can answer the essential question, "How will these students be different—what will they know, understand, be able to do?" What dispositions will they have when they graduate from your high schools (or finish middle school, or leave elementary schools) than they would have been if the gifted program had not existed or they had not participated? Answers to these questions are foundational to determining whether a gifted program is effective in achieving its goals, yet often neither articulated nor evaluated.

Evaluating Programs for Special Populations of Gifted Learners

With the increased attention to groups of learners who have typically been underrepresented in programs for the gifted, and the numerous projects targeting these students through the Javits Gifted and Talented Program, issues surrounding the identification of appropriate program and student goals as well as issues of appropriate techniques for evaluating these programs have emerged. Descriptions of these programs have been provided in such publications as *Contexts for Promise* (Callahan, Tomlinson, & Pizzat, n.d.). As House and Lapan (1994) note, evaluation of these programs presents the same issues as presented in evaluation of all gifted programs, but with an additional layer of issues that emanate from the particular problems in evaluation of any programs that focus on at-risk populations. These include issues of assessment surrounding disadvantaged and limited-English-speaking populations, selection of appropriate indicators (drop-out rates, percentage of students going to college, etc.), and the tenuous nature of gain scores as indicators of success.

Uniquely Applicable Models

Despite the common sense and useful guidelines provided in these articles and in the other parallel articles, book chapters, and monographs, it is notable that all of these principles and models represent adaptations of existing general program evaluation models. The emergence of a new and unique model has not yet occurred. Whether such an evolution is necessary cannot be answered definitively, but we might ask whether such a model might be the stimulus for more widespread acceptance and use of evaluation as an integral part of program planning in gifted education.

Models That Integrate Qualitative and Quantitative Approaches

It is also noticeable that the field has yet to present a clear and useable set of guidelines for the integration of quantitative and qualitative data collection and analysis. Barnette (1983) described naturalistic approaches to gifted and talented program evaluation and Lundsteen (1987) presents a research model with an ethnographic base as a potential model. Lundsteen has articulated the importance of qualitative approaches in helping understand the patterns and interactions within a program, which affect program efficiency and potency. Yet, the field has not built upon this work, nor has it provided careful guidance and illustrations in implementation of the qualitative approach, which can easily be misused, and subsequently, disregarded as too subjective if not correctly implemented.

Nor has the field generated a range of solutions to the issues that arise in determining whether program interventions have had an appreciable effect on student growth and development. Carter (1992) offered one model to address the problems in creating a true experimental approach to gifted program evaluation; however the models currently offered represent adaptations of general models rather than models specifically designed to address the many unique issues that have been raised about evaluating programs for the gifted.

CONCLUSION

It appears that the work of evaluation is not yet finished and many challenges still remain to be addressed by researchers and evaluators. The paucity of application of the knowledge we have and the holes in the research base create the opportunity for experts to make valuable contributions to increased effectiveness and efficiency of programs for the gifted.

REFERENCES

Avery, L. D., VanTassel-Baska, J., & O'Neill, B. (1997). Making evaluation work: One school district's experience. *Gifted Child Quarterly, 41*(4), 124-132. **[See Vol. 11, p. 61.]**

Baker, E. L., & Schacter, J. (1996). Expert benchmarks for student academic performance: The case for gifted children. *Gifted Child Quarterly, 40*(2), 61-65. **[See Vol. 11, p. 109.]**

Barnette, J. J. (1983). Naturalistic approaches to gifted and talented program evaluation. *Journal for the Education of the Gifted, 7*(1), 26-37.

Callahan, C. M. (1986). Asking the right questions: The central issue in evaluating programs for the gifted and talented. *Gifted Child Quarterly, 30*(1), 38-42. **[See Vol. 11, p. 1.]**

Callahan, C. M., & Caldwell, M. S. (1995). *A practitioner's guide to evaluating programs for the gifted.* Washington, DC: National Association for Gifted Children.

Callahan, C. M., & Caldwell, M. S. (1986). Defensible evaluations of programs for the gifted. In C. J. Maker (Ed.), *Critical issues in gifted education* (pp 277-296). Rockville, MD: Aspen.

Callahan, C. M., Tomlinson, C. A., Hunsaker, S. L., Bland, L. C., & Moon, T. (1995). Instruments and evaluation design used in gifted programs. (RM 95132). Storrs, CT: The National Research Center on the Gifted and Talented, University of Connecticut.

Callahan, C. M., Tomlinson, C. A., & Pizzat, P.M. (n.d.). *Context for promise: Practices and innovations in the identification of gifted students.* Charlottesville, VA: University of Virginia.

Carter, K. (1992). A model for evaluating programs for the gifted under non-experimental conditions. *Journal for the Education of the Gifted, 15*(3), 266-283.

Carter, K. R., & Hamilton, W. (1985). Formative evaluation of gifted programs: A process and model. *Gifted Child Quarterly, 29*(1), 5-11. **[See Vol. 11, p. 13.]**

Gallagher, J. J. (1979). Issues in education for the gifted. In Passow, A. H. (Ed.), *The gifted and talented: Their education and development. The seventy-eighth yearbook of the National Society for the Study of Education* (pp. 28-44). Chicago: University of Chicago.

Hertzog, N. B. (2003). Impact of gifted programs from the students' perspectives. *Gifted Child Quarterly, 47*(2), 131-143.

House, E. R., & Lapan, S. (1994). Evaluation of programs for disadvantaged gifted students. *Journal for the Education of the Gifted, 17*(4), 441-446.

Hunsaker, S. L., & Callahan, C. M. (1993). Evaluation of gifted programs: Current practices. *Journal for the Education of the Gifted, 16*(2), 190-200.

Joint Committee on Standards for Educational Evaluation. (1981). *Standards for evaluations of educational programs.* New York: McGraw-Hill.

Kulieke, M. J. (1986). The role of evaluation in inservice and staff development for educators of the gifted. *Gifted Child Quarterly, 30*(3), 140-144. **[See Vol. 11, p. 29.]**

Landrum, M. S. (2001). An evaluation of the catalyst program: Consultation and collaboration in gifted education. *Gifted Child Quarterly, 45*(2), 139-151. **[See Vol. 11, p. 77.]**

Landrum, M. S., Callahan, C. M., & Shaklee, B. D. (2001). *Aiming for excellence: Gifted program standards.* Waco, TX: Prufrock.

Lundsteen, S. W. (1987). Qualitative assessment of gifted education. *Gifted Child Quarterly, 31*(1), 25-29. **[See Vol. 11, p. 119.]**

Martinson, R. A. (1976). *A guide toward better teaching for the gifted.* Ventura, CA: Office of the Ventura County Superintendent of Schools.

Reis, S. M., & Renzulli, J. S. (1991). The assessment of creative products in programs for gifted and talented students. *Gifted Child Quarterly, 35*(3), 128-134. **[See Vol. 11, p. 47.]**

Renzulli, J. S. (1975). *A guidebook for evaluating programs for the gifted and talented.* Ventura, CA: Office of the Ventura County Superintendent of Schools.

Renzulli, J.S., & Ward, V.S. (1969). *Diagnostic and evaluative scales for differential education of the gifted.* Unpublished manuscript. University of Virginia.

VanTassel-Baska, J., Willis, G. B., & Meyer, D. (1989). Evaluation of a full-time self-contained class for gifted students. *Gifted Child Quarterly, 33*(1), 7-10. **[See Vol. 11, p. 101.]**

Wiggins, G. (1996). Anchoring assessment with exemplars: Why students and teachers need models. *Gifted Child Quarterly, 40*(2), 66-69. **[See Vol. 11, p. 39.]**

Asking the Right Questions: The Central Issue in Evaluating Programs for the Gifted and Talented

Carolyn M. Callahan

University of Virginia

What is an appropriate focus for gifted program evaluation? How can we justify focusing program evaluations on questions connected to improving the program rather than judging its success? The author suggests and justifies criteria for framing evaluation questions.

Editor's Note: From Callahan, C. M. (1986). Asking the right questions: The central issue in evaluating programs for the gifted and talented. *Gifted Child Quarterly, 30*(1), 38-42. © 1986 National Association for Gifted Children. Reprinted with permission.

Within every field of scholarly inquiry the most significant advances have come from the inquirer's unique ability to ask different and extending questions, to focus on the appropriate hypotheses and to select a strategy that most effectively and accurately answers the questions posed. The field of evaluation theory and practice is no exception. If the evaluation of gifted and talented programs is to yield valid assessment data and is to have a significant impact on the improvement of gifted programs then more serious attention must be directed toward framing evaluation questions that address the **relevant**, **useful** and **important** issues facing programs.

RELEVANCY, USEFULNESS AND IMPORTANCE

The concepts of relevancy, usefulness and importance are at the core of the problems facing the development of significant evaluation questions. Relevancy refers to the degree to which the questions actually address the functioning of the program under consideration, its components, its activities, its goals, and its structure. Evaluation questions are *not* research questions. Our purpose is *not* to address generalizability, but to address specificity—to the program under consideration. We do not seek to validate a universal identification system; we wish to validate the effectiveness and efficiency of a given system for identifying the students appropriate for a given program. Useful questions provide data that some audience can actually use in the process of making decisions about a program. To know that students failed to achieve specified objectives is more useful data if we can also identify problems in the curriculum or delivery which might be remedied. Important questions yield data helpful in making decisions which will have impact.

ISSUES/CONSTRAINTS IN IDENTIFYING APPROPRIATE EVALUATION QUESTIONS

In the formulation of evaluation questions for gifted and talented programs, one is faced with a particular set of issues/constraints which overlap those of all other education programs, another set of issues which are shared in the evaluation of any special project and then a set of issues unique to the evaluation of programs for the gifted.

Similarities to the evaluation of programs for other exceptionalities. Like programs for the handicapped, many programs for the gifted are predicated on the development of individualized programs of study, on the establishment of goals which are particular to the interests and abilities of the individual child, e.g., Renzulli's Enrichment Triad Model (1977) and Renzulli and Smith's Individualized Educational Programs for the Gifted (1979). In such programs it is unreasonable to set group behavioral objectives against which one can assess accomplishment. In addition, the provision of programs for a special population makes the establishment of control groups which can be used as a comparison a very difficult, and sometimes impossible, task. Ethical and political considerations nearly always dictate that all eligible children be served.

Unique issues in evaluating program for the gifted. Unlike programs for other exceptional students, programs for the gifted and talented face the difficulty of setting standards of performance against which achievement can be measured, or even against which program operation can be judged. First of all, the kinds of programs offered to gifted students vary considerably from school to school and no agreed upon standards of good programming exist within the field of gifted education for use in establishing criteria for specific program functioning. Secondly, many of the objectives in programs for the gifted are very complex and not easily defined. For example, the concepts of creativity and critical thinking are hypothetical constructs whose definitions have been the subject of much debate in psychology for twenty years. Furthermore, there are no empirical studies which provide norms or guidelines for "expected growth" over a specified time period in either the traditional academic areas or the more unique areas such as critical thinking, creativity, or higher level thinking skills. Therefore, it is unsound practice to phrase evaluation questions in terms of expectations of the attainment of certain gains on a specific achievement test.

An even more fundamental issue in phrasing questions when evaluating programs for the gifted is the validity issue. Validity of both the questions asked and the instruments selected to use in gathering data relative to these questions are often not given serious consideration in the development of evaluation designs. First, why is this a particular problem in evaluating programs for the gifted? The reasons lie in the uniqueness of the types of goals and objectives set for these programs. Because many goals of gifted and talented programs are both product oriented and individualized, we often must reject altogether questions phrased in terms of test score gains because paper and pencil assessments simply will not validly assess the program's goals. For example, a goal of developing independent study skills and the use of alternative resources is often translated into a question focusing on gains on a "Use of Sources" subtest of a standardized achievement test. Whereas the program staff intended to develop students' abilities to identify appropriate new, non-standard sources, to use a variety of types of resources and to use more sophisticated resources, the tests assess students' ability to use an index or table of contents. Second, many of the statements of goals and objectives of programs for the gifted tend to be holistic and long-term, making their evaluation very difficult and often resulting in the formulation of very short term, but invalid evaluation questions. If, in fact, these short term questions relate to enabling objectives then collection of data about those issues will be useful. But too often we stop at the point of evaluating students' increased fluency scores and fail to examine completely the question of an increase in creative productivity. Or we evaluate whether or not identification procedures were carried out as prescribed but fail to evaluate whether *gifted* students were actually identified by those procedures.

Issues common to all educational program evaluation. The last major issue is neither new nor unique to gifted programs. That is the issue of the *focus* of the evaluation and the questions which emerge from that focus. This issue was first addressed in depth in the field of evaluating programs for the gifted and talented by Renzulli (1975). Bemoaning the generation of evaluation questions which focused only on end products of programming efforts and which tended to use inappropriate standards for judging the quality of gifted program activities, he pointed to the importance of constructing both formative and summative evaluation questions and questions relating to process, product and presage information. His comments reflected the need not simply to judge a program as "successful" or "unsuccessful," but to help identify those aspects of a program which were functioning as they should and, therefore, would be likely to contribute to a successful program.

CURRENT DIRECTIONS

The current direction taken by evaluation theorists and practitioners is to extend these ideas further by expanding on the *purposes* of program evaluation in order to address the relevancy, utility and importance issues mentioned above. The practice of formulating evaluation questions using an expanded concept of the purposes of evaluation originates from the time that Scriven (1967), Stufflebeam (1968), and Stake (1967) first began exploring the concept of evaluation as the process of gathering data for the purpose of decision-making. Up until that time, evaluation paradigms had most often mimicked research paradigms. Both evaluators and those being evaluated tended to think only in terms of very reductionistic, experimentally phrased and outcome oriented evaluation questions such as: Did the students become better independent learners as a result of this instructional program? Are the teachers using questions which require higher level thinking as a result of the staff development program? etc.

Although such outcome questions legitimately remain one of the foci of evaluation efforts, the work of the late 1960's and the 1970's began a trend in evaluation directed toward asking questions and providing information which are of greater utility to the program being evaluated, to increasing communication and to addressing those issues fundamental to program planning. The application of these expanded purposes to the evaluation of programs for the gifted and talented has been elaborated on by Callahan and Caldwell (in press) and include: documentation of the need for a program, documentation of the case for a particular approach, documentation of the feasibility of a program, documentation of program implementation, identification of program strengths and weaknesses, provision of data for inprogress revisions of the program, documentation of the results or impacts of the program, and explanation and description of the program to interested and uninformed audiences. Each of these program purposes may serve as the basis for the generation of a unique set of evaluation concerns and questions depending on the context of the evaluation and the audience to be served (see Audiences). Questions derived from these evaluation purposes address specific program outcomes in the minority of cases. More often they address the process of describing and explaining a program, provide information rather than value judgments, and leave the evaluation process open to input according to the needs of the program.

New methodologies. The introduction of new methodologies borrowed from the social science research arena (e.g., ethnographic research borrowed from cultural anthropology) (Guba, 1978) has also contributed to a dramatic revision of the types of evaluation questions posed as well as to the fundamental approach to evaluation. Because these "naturalistic" approaches differ from traditional methodologies in philosophical base, inquiry paradigm, purpose, framework/ design, style, view of reality, value structure, setting, scope, context, conditions, treatment definition, and methods (Guba, 1978), it is inevitable that the questions which emerge from designs based on these methodologies will differ from traditional modes of inquiry. For example, naturalistic methodologies tend to be emergent and variable in nature rather than preordinate and fixed. Thus an evaluator who is applying a naturalistic strategy may or may not start an investigation with a series of specifically stated hypotheses (evaluation questions), but it is almost inevitable that the process of studying the program will yield new questions and new strategies for answering those questions as the investigator uncovers new information. An individual pursuing a non-traditional education approach would be likely to phrase evaluation questions in a more general, open-ended manner.

At the risk of oversimplifying the process of naturalistic inquiry and exaggerating the distinctions between qualitative and quantitative methodologies, the following is offered as an example of the contrasting questions which emerge. A traditional evaluation design might pose the question: "Do the scheduling process and curricular adaptations reflect the individual needs of gifted students?" A traditional evaluator is likely to define the "need" very specifically and may focus on aptitude as the variable to consider. The methodology selected may be to rate student programs on the degree of individualization in student records (programs) and to present students with surveys to complete. A naturalistic inquirer would probably begin with a question more like: "On what bases are the schedules and curricula for gifted students modified? Are student needs being met by these modifications?" It would then be appropriate to conduct in-depth interviews with students, teachers, counselors, parents and administrators. In the process, one individual might mention that "Yes, my schedule is different, but it's not what I *want* to do." The evaluator's question may then become, "Are relevant variables (i.e., student interest in this case) being considered as part of the scheduling process?"

Phrasing of evaluation questions. The phrasing of the evaluation questions also suggest the difference between the traditional evaluation questions and the more current notions of evaluation. The differences between the type of question asked for research purposes and one asked for evaluation purposes are those of generalizability and those described by Yavorsky (1984) as a distinction between asking "How should a program be planned to work?" and "How well is the planned program working?"

Audiences. The audience(s) to be served by the evaluation is also a key factor in determining the appropriate evaluation questions. As Dinham and Udall (in press) point out, the purpose of evaluation should be formed by looking at the specific needs of specific audiences. It follows that the evaluation questions should focus on issues which are of specific relevance and importance to specific audiences. Yavorsky (1984) identifies two distinct groups of audiences when she gives directions for the selection of appropriate evaluation concerns—external and internal audiences. External audiences consist of such individuals and groups as funding agencies (local, state or federal government; private foundations, etc.), higher levels of administration, professional associations and certification agencies, consumer agencies (e.g., parent groups), community and assorted interest groups. Internal audiences are those which are directly involved with the functioning of the program and would include such groups as program administrators, teachers in the program and in the school division, central office and building administrators, students in the program, etc.

It is likely that the interests of each of these groups would overlap to some degree and the same evaluation question may provide information to a variety of audiences. For example, those individuals who work very closely with the students (program staff, regular classroom teachers, parents, etc.) will identify questions that relate to the impact of the program on the student both academically and psychologically. On occasion, however, different audiences have very different information needs. Funding agents and administrators often express different concerns than staff, parents and students—concerns about the cost of the program.

It is important that an evaluation designer give all relevant audiences the opportunity to voice their evaluation concerns and questions. Renzulli (1975) suggests the use of an input questionnaire and interviews. His recommendation is that any audience which is either directly involved in the program (students, parents, staff) or indirectly involved (non-program staff, counselors, etc.) should have the opportunity to raise concerns, to suggest questions that should be addressed, and to voice their opinion about types of information that should be collected in evaluating the program.

There may also be concerns and questions which should be addressed even though they may not be specifically mentioned by one of the audiences addressed in the original evaluation planning. For example, one should consider the kinds of data such as unintended outcomes as described by Scriven (1967) when he talks of goal-free evaluation. In the process of examining effects of a computer class on gifted students one may uncover telltale grumbling by other teachers that this class interferes with the equal access to computers that they believe all students should have or one may discover that assignments in other courses are left incomplete. It can be predicted that such situations, if not addressed, will have negative impacts on the continuation of the class. Even though no audience might have anticipated such a situation, it is important to attend to such evidence even though it was not included in the original planning.

Several of the evaluation paradigms mentioned earlier as part of the group labeled naturalistic inquiry have potential for addressing specific audience needs as well as uncovering new questions. For example the Responsive Model of Stake (1975) "orients more directly to program activities than to program intents" and "responds to audience requirements for information" (p. 14). Other models mentioned by Guba which seem to fall in the same category are the Judicial Model (Wolf, 1975), the Transactional Model (Talmadge, 1975), the Connoisseurship Model (Eisner, 1979), and the Illumination Model (Parlett and Hamilton, 1976).

THE IMPORTANCE OF PROGRAM DESCRIPTION IN FORMULATING EVALUATION QUESTIONS

Reaching the point where we can identify questions which are, in fact, audience responsive, appropriate for assessing the functioning and goals of gifted programs, and measurable is dependent on being able to describe the program. Experience in evaluating programs for the gifted demonstrates very quickly that one cannot evaluate what one cannot describe.

The most thorough consideration of all possible evaluation questions will result if care is taken to describe the program in terms of its components (e.g., identification process, management, curriculum and instructional strategies, programming options, etc.), the functional relationships between these components, the resources which support each component, the activities of each component, and the expected outcomes of the activities carried out as a function of each component. (See Yavorsky, 1984). If the evaluator and program administrator can identify each of the aforementioned attributes of the program, then evaluation questions will naturally emerge. Further evaluation questions should emerge from an examination of this description by those other audiences who have a need for evaluative data. Very simple questioning by the evaluator should yield a list of areas in which individuals and groups can reflect their concerns.

GUIDELINES FOR FORMULATING EVALUATION QUESTIONS

Guidelines for formulating the evaluation questions from these concerns *and* prioritizing questions are suggested by Yavorsky (1984). The first of these guidelines is to construct and give priority to questions of concern to internal and external audiences. The second is to attend to questions relating to areas of the program that are of central functional importance. That is, success of the program is highly dependent on the success of that component. Third, one should identify questions that are suggestive of problems. These are often generated around areas that are not well defined, where program design is in question or is in controversy, where there has been a history of problems—either in that particular program or gifted programs in general, or areas marked by staff disagreement. Finally, one should identify those questions where information is needed soon.

Covert (personal communication, July 5, 1985) suggests that one also should generate questions relative to the adequacy and availability of resources which are needed to execute the program, the adequacy of planned activities, the degree to which implementation follows plans or is appropriately modified, and the degree to which the components of a program are in accord with one another and operate as a unit. Questions of resources are important in helping programs deliver what is expected or identifying reasons why the program fails to deliver. For example, if the identification of a musically talented student is dependent on past performance and the school has no regular music program, then identification is a more difficult and expensive process. Questions of the adequacy of planned activities are important for helping prevent unnecessary failures. If one can identify faulty logic in planning, a considerable savings in time and energy are possible. If administrative staff development does not precede teacher staff development, the effectiveness of the latter may be seriously impaired. Questions of implementation are necessary to determine whether the achievement of expected outcomes (or lack of achievement) is attributable to the program as planned. Questions of accord are necessary to help identify potentially conflicting plans or implementation problems. A school may plan for students to engage in a mentor program but so tightly schedule advanced placement classes that students have no opportunity to participate.

Guba (1978) points out that the naturalistic evaluator is "materially assisted by keeping in mind that there are certain standard situations in which the persons involved may see the entity being evaluated as giving rise to issues or concerns" (p. 51). Among those he lists are:

- Undesirable consequences of an interaction or course of action (Parents may feel that a resource room may have a negative effect on other students' self concepts.)
- Confusion regarding courses of action (Teachers may not understand their role in the identification process.)
- An undesirable deviation from older practice (After all, the regular classroom was good enough for me.)
- Conflicts with traditional values (The gifted program may be perceived as contrary to the "American value of equal education.")
- Conflicts with personal values (Activities focusing on social issues in a gifted program may conflict with community values.)

- Potential loss of power (Principals may see the coordinator of gifted programs as having too much authority over the teachers in his or her building.)
- Potential economic threats (Teachers of regular classrooms may perceive that the resource room drains resources from the regular class instruction.)
- Perceived inconsistency with a suggested course of action (If the classroom teachers recommended a resource room program and the school chose to deliver instruction in a cluster group arrangement, the teachers are likely to be disgruntled and perhaps less cooperative.)
- Lack of understanding of rationales or goals (If a teacher does not understand the goals of program, he or she will not be effective in implementing the curriculum.)
- Bias based on a negative personal experience with a given institution (Just one example of a student who was not successful in an accelerated school program can seriously tarnish the image of acceleration programs in general.)
- Potentially harmful side effects (Does being in the gifted program result in a negative influence on social interactions?)

An additional factor which should influence the selection of evaluation questions is the degree to which the question is "answerable." Unfortunately, in the field of evaluation of gifted programs we usually find two, equally unacceptable, ways of dealing with this factor. On the one hand, we find ourselves answering only very simple, easy to answer but relatively insignificant or narrow questions because there are available instruments or because data can be collected easily. For example, we often find evaluation studies focusing only on student, parent and teacher perceptions of programs or curriculum as indicated on questionnaires. The narrowness of the evaluation questions posed in these studies results in a tendency to ignore halo effects, failure to gather in-depth information on what influences the perceptions of the individuals responding, and failure to verify actual changes or outcomes of program activities.

This is not to suggest that perceptions are unimportant; rather we must consider whether perceptions in and of themselves are sufficient evidence for good decision making. At the other extreme, the evaluator of gifted programs sometimes asks questions at either such a complex or undefined level that it is virtually impossible to find strategies to evaluate the program because the questions do not lend themselves to assessment or documentation.

Evaluation questions have also been limited by the inability of evaluators to look at alternative data sources such as objective and subjective product assessment (performance rating scales, essay ratings, independent project ratings, etc.) The tradition of assessing impacts on the basis of multiple-choice test items severely limits the kinds of evaluation evidence we can gather and transmit to interested parties. Renzulli and Reis (1985) and Callahan (1983) have offered product rating scales which provide alternatives for gifted and talented student product ratings.

One final extension of evaluation questions that should be considered is into the realm of cost effectiveness/cost benefit analysis (CEA/CBA). It is important that we raise questions about the misleading conclusions that can be drawn by simply stating that programs produced statistically significant changes in the students. In times of limited funding for special programs, it is important that we consider the factors of cost relative to the benefit to students in evaluating programs.

A DIRECTION FOR FURTHER RESEARCH

One final note on the issue of evaluation questions as it relates to this special issue of *Gifted Child Quarterly*. This brief piece does not address the issues of research in the area of program evaluation. In fact, the topic of evaluation research (as opposed to the practice of program evaluation) is a distinct topic and practically non-existent in the field of gifted education. The paradigms for evaluation which have been described and implemented in the literature in the education of the gifted and talented are drawn largely from the more general field of program evaluation and have not been subject to rigorous tests of usefulness, generalizability, impact, etc. that characterize the field of research. There is, therefore, a need to more closely and systematically examine the kinds of evaluation questions asked in terms of their relevance (as perceived by the audiences), their usefulness (as evidenced by actual decision-making based on evaluation findings), and their importance (as determined by the judgments of experts, the program and school administration, the staff of the program, etc.).

The topic of evaluation questions is not and cannot be an entirely independent issue. One must consider the evaluation question in light of the design or paradigm which has been selected for the evaluation. And this is a "Which comes first—the chicken or egg?" question in evaluation. Do we formulate questions and then choose a design or do we choose a design and allow the questions to emerge from our design approach? It is most important to remember the mutual dependencies and collect and report data which acknowledges the interrelationships.

REFERENCES

Callahan, C. M. (1983). Issues in evaluating programs for the gifted. *Gifted Child Quarterly, 27*(1), 3–7.

Callahan, C. M., & Caldwell, M. S. (in press) Defensible evaluations of programs for the gifted. In C. J. Maker (Ed.), *Critical issues in gifted education*. Rockville, MD: Aspen.

Dinham, S. M., & Udall, A. S. (in press) Evaluation for gifted education: Synthesis and discussion. In C. J. Maker (Ed.), *Critical issues in gifted education*. Rockville, MD: Aspen.

Eisner, Elliot (1979). *The educational imagination*. New York: Macmillan.

Guba, E. G. (1978). Toward a methodology of naturalistic inquiry in educational evaluation. *CSE Monograph Series in Evaluation, 8.*

Parlett, M., & Hamilton, D. (1976). Evaluation as illumination: A new approach to the study of innovatory programs. In G. V. Glass (Ed.), *Evaluation studies review annual* (Volume 1). Beverly Hills, CA: Sage Publications.

Renzulli, J. S. (1975). *Working draft: A guidebook for evaluating programs for the gifted and talented.* Ventura, CA: Office of the Ventura County Superintendent of Schools.

Renzulli, J. S. (1977). *The enrichment triad model: A guide for developing defensible programs for the gifted and talented.* Mansfield Center, CT: Creative Learning Press.

Renzulli, J. S. & Reis, S. M. (1985). *The schoolwide enrichment model.* Mansfield Center, CT: Creative Learning Press.

Renzulli, J. S., & Smith, L. H. (1979). *A guidebook for developing individualized educational programs for gifted and talented students.* Mansfield Center, CT: Creative Learning Press.

Scriven, M. (1967). The methodology of evaluation. In R. E. Stake (Ed.), *Curriculum evaluation* (American Educational Research Association monograph series on evaluation, No. 1). Chicago: Rand McNally.

Stake, R. E. (1967). The countenance of educational evaluation. *Teachers College Record, 68,* 523–540.

Stake, R. E. (1975). Program evaluation, particularly responsive evaluation (Occasional Paper No. 5). The Evaluation Center, Western Michigan University.

Stufflebeam, D. L. (1968). *Evaluation as enlightenment for decision-making.* Columbus, Ohio: Evaluation Center, Ohio State University.

Talmadge, H. (1975). Evaluation of local school community problems: A transactional evaluation approach. *Journal of Research and Development in Education, 8,* 32–41.

Wolf, R. L. (1975). Trial by jury: A new evaluation method. *Phi Delta Kappan, 1975, 57.*

Yavorsky, D. K. (1984). *Discrepancy evaluation: A practitioner's guide.* Charlottesville, VA: University of Virginia, Curry School of Education Evaluation Research Center.

2

Formative Evaluation of Gifted Programs: A Process and Model

Kyle R. Carter

University of Northern Colorado

Wilma Hamilton

Weld County School District, Greeley, Colorado

The authors suggest that the recent focus on excellence in public education will lead to an increase in the evaluation of gifted programs. They maintain that evaluation of gifted programs should be formative, as opposed to summative, because gifted programming serves a valuable social need. The authors describe the process that evaluators go through to conduct a program evaluation, and then present their program evaluation model. Two approaches are integrated in their model. First, process-oriented evaluation defines essential program components and standards of acceptance. Second, outcome-oriented evaluation assesses components via student outcomes. Both approaches are described and suggestions are given for their use.

Editor's Note: From Carter, K. R., & Hamilton, W. (1985). Formative evaluation of gifted programs: A process and model. *Gifted Child Quarterly, 29*(1), 5-11. © 1985 National Association for Gifted Children. Reprinted with permission.

The 1980s have been a particularly difficult time for public education. The decline of fiscal resources has forced school boards to make difficult budget trimming decisions. Since gifted programs are sometimes regarded as educational frills by board members, gifted and talented programs are often targets of budget cutting (see Mitchell, 1984). Those recommending the elimination of gifted programs typically believe the gifted can reach their potential without special help. Unfortunately, they must be unaware of the findings of the Marland Report (1972), or else they choose to ignore Marland's warning:

> ... research has confirmed that many talented children perform far below their intellectual potential. We are increasingly being stripped of the comfortable notion that a bright mind will make its own way. Intellectual and creative talent cannot survive educational neglect and apathy. (p. 9)

In the face of this budget cutting, it seems clear that proponents of gifted education must demonstrate that gifted children need differentiated education in order to reach their potential.

Fiscal problems have been encountered amidst recent reports alleging mediocrity in American education. These reports may have an impact on the funding of gifted programs at the local level. A case in point is the report by the President's Commission on Teaching Excellence entitled, "A Nation at Risk" (1983). This report was highly critical of public education's ability to prepare American students for competition in the industrialized world. Authors of the report called for sweeping changes in the educational system, including increased programming to meet the needs of the gifted student. Other national reports have also supported programming for gifted students. They include "Action for Excellence" (1983) sponsored by the Education Commission of the United States, "Education and Economic Progress" (1983) sponsored by the Carnegie Corporation, and "High School: A Report on Secondary Education in America" by Boyer (1983), sponsored by The Carnegie Foundation.

The recent reports on public education are both a source of support and a challenge to those in gifted education. They provide support because they echo the feelings expressed in the Marland Report more than a decade ago: The gifted are a national resource that is being wasted and educational programs should be developed to utilize this resource. On the other hand, the report is a challenge to gifted educators. The authors of the reports imply that gifted programs must be of high quality and demonstrate their effectiveness.

As a result of the fiscal crisis in public education and reports of mediocrity in our schools, the public has become sensitized to issues of both funding and quality related to educational programs. In the future, it is unlikely that school boards will fund gifted programs because they appear to be a good idea. To fund or not to fund will depend more and more on program effectiveness, as measured by student outcomes.

Program evaluations will increase in the years ahead, i.e., long established, valued gifted programs will be evaluated to determine their effectiveness and to identify areas where improvements can be made. New programs for the gifted will be evaluated for the purpose of demonstrating their effectiveness and working out problems that will be an inevitable part of the first year. In either case, program evaluation information will help to inform school personnel, school boards, and the general public about the nature and effect of these programs.

The paper describes an evaluation process and model that was developed by the authors to help the school district in Greeley, Colorado, assess the effectiveness of its gifted and talented program. The steps of the process and the model will be explained and suggestions for its use will be given. It is the hope of the authors that this model will assist others in planning and conducting evaluations of gifted programs.

EVALUATION PHILOSOPHY

Scriven (1967) labeled program evaluation either summative or formative. Summative evaluations are characterized by assessment of the *outcomes of established* programs in determining their overall effectiveness. Presumably, the results of the evaluation are then used to determine whether or not the program will continue to exist. On the other hand, formative evaluations are conducted to *improve* new programs in *transition*. The emphasis in this type of evaluation is improvement.

In interpreting Scriven's two types of evaluations, Cronbach (1982) expands the concept of formative evaluation to include the measurement of program outcomes for the purpose of program improvement. The overriding assumption of Cronbach's conception of formative evaluation is that the program addresses a significant social need and will continue to exist. As Cronbach (1982) points out, "to cut off a program without substituting an alternative is to abandon the commitment to alleviate the social problem in question" (p. 13).

The philosophy underlying the evaluation model described in this paper is similar to Cronbach's conception of formative evaluation. First, it is assumed that gifted programs serve an important social need and thus should continue to exist. Second, the focus of the model is on anticipated program outcomes. Program effectiveness is judged on the basis of these outcomes and when weaknesses are identified, the model provides for program improvement.

EVALUATION PROCESS

Figure 1 shows the process the authors used to evaluate the Greeley gifted and talented program. This section describes an overview of that process.

A meeting is held with the *decision maker* to determine the purpose, scope, and general expectations of the evaluation. The decision maker is an individual or a group of individuals who have overall administrative responsibility for the program. During that meeting, the evaluators must make certain that their perceptions of the evaluation are consistent with those of the decision maker. The parties involved must make clear what they both mean by evaluation, the intended purpose of the evaluation, the program elements to be evaluated, reasonable approaches for carrying out the evaluation, and the standards to be used in judging program quality. Nevo (1983) suggests conceptualizing evaluations around 10 dimensions, represented by the following questions:

How is evaluation defined?
   What are the functions of evaluation?
   What are the objects of evaluation?
   What kinds of information should be collected regarding each object?
   What criteria should be used to judge the merit and worth of an evaluated object?
   Who should be served by an evaluation?
   What is the process of doing an evaluation?
   What methods of inquiry should be used in evaluation?
   Who should do evaluation?
   By what standards should evaluation be judged?

Program evaluators will find the Nevo article helpful because his answer to each question provides a summary of the viewpoints of experts in program evaluation along each of the 10 dimensions.

At times, the decision maker will have a clear objective in mind when initiating an evaluation. If this is the case, the evaluation team will be told which program objects to evaluate. However, at other times the decision makers may not have a clear idea about the evaluation. Instead, they will rely on the evaluation team for the *identification of potential program objects*. When this occurs, the evaluation team has two sources from which it can identify evaluation objects. First, the evaluation team may solicit input from various *target groups* who have an interest in the program. Examples of target groups include parents of gifted students, gifted students, teachers of the gifted, and principals. Second, the team may suggest evaluating one or more of those program elements essential for a G/T program (see Table 1).

Since most evaluations are limited in some respect by money, time, or personnel, decision makers usually have to make a choice regarding those program objects that are to be a part of the evaluation and those that must wait. *Selecting objects* is a collaborative effort between the evaluation team and the decision makers. Priorities are determined in relation to the purpose of the evaluation, as well as time and money constraints.

When objects have been selected, the evaluation team *selects criteria* that are suitable for making judgments about the evaluation objects. These criteria must fit within the overall evaluation framework, as determined during the initial

Figure 1   A formative evaluation process for the evaluation of gifted and talented
programs

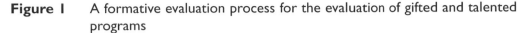

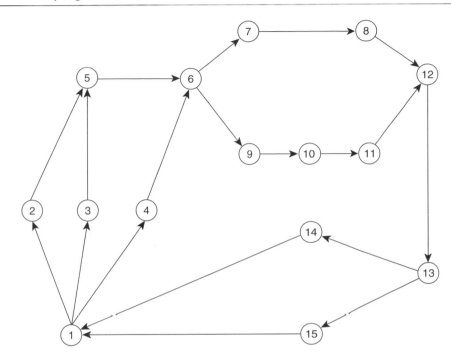

ACTIVITY OR PROCEDURE

1. Hold meeting with decision maker to plan evaluation.
2. Identify potential evaluation objects from program elements.
3. Identify potential evaluation objects from target group input.
4. Decision maker identifies objects of evaluation.
5. Select objects in consultation with decision maker.
6. Select criteria in consultation with decision maker.
7. Choose qualitative criteria (process-oriented) in consultation with decision maker.
8. Conduct content analysis.
9. Choose quantitative criteria (outcome-oriented) in consultation with decision maker.
10. Develop research design.
11. Collect and analyze data.
12. Write report of findings.
13. Obtain decision maker's response.
14. Develop program components found to be deficient.
15. Improve evaluation procedures and measures found to be faulty.

meeting with the decision maker. Specifically, evaluators must choose criteria
that are deemed by the decision maker as being reasonable and practical measures
of the evaluation objects.

The selection of criteria will determine the approach the evaluation team
will follow. If the criteria are *outcome-oriented* then the evaluation will be more
empirical, utilizing a *research design* that requires data collection and *analysis*.

Table 1   Essential Components of a Gifted and Talented Program

Definition
Philosophy
Identification Procedures and Criteria
Program Goals and Objectives
Student Goals and Objectives
Curriculum
Personnel
Budget
Program Evaluation

Experimental, quasi-experimental (see Campbell & Stanley, 1963), and descriptive designs are all possible methods of this process. If criteria are more *process-oriented*, the evaluator uses a qualitative approach. Existing written documents about evaluation objects are inspected and evaluated against predetermined standards. This process, called a *content analysis* (Borg & Gall, 1983), helps answer such questions as, "Are the program goals adequate?" or "Does the program have a clearly defined curriculum?"

The *findings* and *recommendations* of the evaluation are communicated to the decision maker(s). Since the evaluation itself is a formative process, i.e., emphasizing program improvement, recommendations typically call for *program development* or modifications in the evaluation process. Once these changes have been made, the decision maker may call for continued evaluation, beginning again the cycle of program evaluation.

THE MODEL

All gifted and talented programs can be analyzed into essential program elements. As conceptualized by the authors, a complete G/T program must include the elements shown in Table 1. As previously stated, criteria for evaluating these objects may be either qualitative or quantitative. The proposed model suggests criteria and methods for evaluating each program element. If the criteria are qualitative, the model proposes a process-oriented evaluation, termed "content analysis." When criteria are quantitative, an outcomes-oriented evaluation is used. The process approach will be described first, followed by the outcomes approach.

Process-Oriented Evaluation: Content Analysis

The authors have reviewed various writings (e.g., Fox, 1979; Gallagher, 1975, 1979b; Marland, 1972) and concluded that well-defined gifted programs have the following program elements clearly articulated: a definition, a philosophy, identification procedures and criteria, program goals and objectives, student goals and objectives, a differentiated curriculum, inservice for school personnel and parents, position descriptions of personnel, a budget, and a system for program evaluation. Content analysis, defined as an inspection of existing printed material, is conducted to evaluate each of these program components. A brief description of these components, and the criteria used to assess them, is presented below.

Definition. The definition presented in the Marland Report (1972) has been adopted by many programs. Although Renzulli (1978) and Gallagher (1979a) have been critical of the definition because it fails to operationalize the selection of gifted children, we believe it provides a good beginning point for most new programs for the following reasons. First, the definition is widely-known and accepted by many educators. Second, it defines the major categories of giftedness that are recognized today. Third, each district can identify objective criteria for each category to operationalize the definition.

Most school districts will be unable to serve all categories, due to budget and personnel limitations. Therefore, definitions should be evaluated to determine if the area of giftedness is clearly defined and measurable and if the breadth of the definition (i.e., the number of categories of giftedness) is realistic, as judged by the district resources. Districts should be aware that once definitions of giftedness are adopted as policy, they may be legally responsible for delivering services to *all* individuals specified by the definition. For example, if the USOE definition becomes board policy, any child who meets the criteria for those categories (intelligence, specific academic aptitude, creativity, visual and performing arts, etc.) must be served. Unless a district can afford to provide programs for such large numbers of children, adoption of broad definitions should be avoided. One alternative is to limit definitions to those categories of students in the USOE definition that can be served by district resources.

Philosophy. The statement of philosophy describes the rationale that undergirds the gifted program. It explains why gifted education is considered important to the school district by clearly defining those values and beliefs that make gifted education important. In evaluating the philosophy statement, the program evaluator must determine whether it clearly explains the program rationale and whether this rationale is consistent with the definition.

Identification Procedures and Criteria. Since the identification process operationalizes the program's definition of giftedness, identification procedures must be consistent with the manner in which the gifted are defined. Specifically, identification procedures should be checked to assure that the following guidelines are followed:

1. Identification criteria are specifically related to the definition.

2. Performance indicators are reliable, valid measures of the defined areas of giftedness.

Table 2   An Example of a Program Goal and Its Set of Objectives

PROGRAM GOAL: To develop, implement, and evaluate a continuous (3-12) program for intellectually and creatively gifted students.

PROGRAM OBJECTIVES

The district will . . .

1. specify the student population to be served.
2. articulate the philosophy and justify the existence of the program.
3. outline an identification system consistent with the program's definition and philosophy.
4. provide programmatic models to meet individual student needs

   a. mentorships
   b. pull-out enrichment
   c. enrichment in the regular classroom
   d. advanced placement
   e. honors classes
   f. acceleration.

5. inform, inservice, and involve parents and teachers in aspects of the program related to the child's talents, skills, and abilities.
6. specify the general resources (i.e., funding, materials, mentors, staff) needed to provide services to gifted, creative, and talented students.
7. identify and secure funding outside the school district.
8. promote a positive image to the community

   a. publicize program activities through media
   b. participate in community projects
   c. address local agencies and organizations.

3. Multiple criteria are used.

4. Cutoffs are reasonable in light of relevant research and the amount of error found in each performance indicator.

5. Separate scores have been converted to a common scale and weighted appropriately when composite scores have been computed.

6. The process allows for an appeals procedure.

7. Due process is followed.

8. The entire process reflects the stated program philosophy.

Program Goal(s) and Objectives. The program goals provide overall direction for the program. The goals should be clearly written, feasible, and fit within the overall philosophy of gifted education. Each goal should be made explicit by means of its own set of clearly written objectives. Objectives should be measurable, consistent with program philosophy, and practical. An example of a program goal and its objectives is shown in Table 2.

Table 3   An Example of a Student Goal and Its Set of Objectives

(3rd Grade)
GOAL:THE CONCEPT OF GIFTEDNESS

The student will understand the nature and characteristics of giftedness.	The student will accept giftedness as a valued entity in society.
COGNITIVE OBJECTIVES	*AFFECTIVE OBJECTIVES*

The student will:

1. define giftedness, historically and personally.
2. list characteristics associated with various types of giftedness (i.e., intellectual, creative, psychomotor, etc.).
3. discuss the implications and responsibilities of being gifted (positively, negatively, cross-culturally).
4. describe the process by which specific talents are identified.
5. formulate a statement concerning the responsibilities of giftedness.

The student will:

1. develop an awareness of unique talents, skills, and abilities.
2. appreciate the need for individualized educational programming.

Student Goals and Objectives. Student goals should integrate both cognitive and affective outcomes. Learning theorists have noted that learning occurs along with attitude formation, both positive and negative (Bower & Hilgard, 1981). In fact, learning may reach mastery, even though the student develops negative attitudes toward the subject matter. Thus, students may have similar abilities in a subject area such as mathematics, but they may differ in the degree to which they like it. So educators must purposefully plan to teach positive feelings toward the cognitive skills that are a part of the curriculum. According to Scriven (1966), teachers who avoid teaching cognitive-related values may rightfully be considered professionally incompetent. In commenting on Scriven's remark, Bloom, Madeaus, and Hastings (1981) stated "schools have an obligation to work toward the realization of affective objectives" (p. 298). If one of the long-term goals of public education is life-long learning, then students must value and appreciate the learning process as well as the subject matter. Thus, life-long learning depends upon the integration of cognitive and affective learning.

In evaluating student goals, the evaluator should look for an integration of cognitive and affective outcomes (see Table 3). Each goal should suggest a differentiated curriculum, be clearly written, and consistent with the program philosophy. Each goal should include its own set of objectives, clearly communicating a measurable student outcome.

Curriculum. The curriculum is the heart of each G/T program and will determine whether student goals and objectives are met. The curriculum should be evaluated against the following criteria:

1. The curriculum shows scope and sequence.

2. The curriculum was developed from student goals and objectives.

3. The curriculum is consistent with the philosophy of differentiated education.

In conjunction with the analysis of program content, evaluation must be concerned with various other input factors which impact on the quality of any program. Included here would be such items as personnel and budget considerations.

Inservice for Staff and Parents. Planned inservice activities for staff and parent groups are necessary to educate professionals and the public about the need for gifted programs. Surveys (Marland, 1972; Rubenzer & Twaite, 1979; Gallagher, 1981; Mitchell, 1984) have repeatedly demonstrated ambivalent attitudes toward gifted programs, along with misconceptions. Research by the authors (Carter & Hamilton, 1983) indicate that parents of the gifted, classroom teachers, school principals, and teachers of the gifted desire more inservice on topics such as the gifted curriculum, characteristics of the gifted, and the identification process.

Personnel. The following input factors should be analyzed with regard to a school district's gifted and talented personnel/staff:

1. Professional preparation of the G/T staff (i.e., degrees or preparation in G/T area).

2. Total years of experience in teaching.

3. Number of years in G/T classroom.

4. Amount and continuity of post-degree inservice or training related to G/T education.

5. Prior administrative evaluations.

Budget. Although it is well known that numerous G/T programs function on a "shoestring," while others thrive using federal, state, local, and/or private funding, the evaluator's real questions should revolve around the budget's effect on the quality of such program functioning. For example, in gathering evaluative information, the following budgetary matters should be addressed and analyzed with regard to their possible impact on other program elements (i.e., personnel, curriculum materials, etc.):

1. Utilization of funding sources.

2. Total amount spent per year on G/T programs.

3. Breakdown by category of budget allocations

    a. personnel/staff/coordinator
    b. materials—hardware/software—printing
    c. instructional improvement/staff development
    d. testing
    e. mileage
    f. conferences
    g. substitutes
    h. mentors, speakers, field trips, etc.
    i. program evaluation.

Program Evaluation. Specific procedures and policies should be written to specify a plan for the regular evaluation of each of the G/T program components. Plans should address each of the 10 questions formulated by Nevo presented earlier. In addition, evaluation plans should use process and outcome approaches within a formative evaluation context. The overall goal of the plan should be to provide regular feedback to the decision maker for program improvement.

Outcome-Oriented Evaluation

The outcome-oriented approach to evaluation is designed to determine whether programs produce the results they were designed to produce. The effectiveness of program elements is judged against expected outcomes. Thus, the only requirement for an outcome-oriented evaluation is that the expectations of program elements must be specified, usually in the form of program objectives. If objectives are present, the evaluator can then proceed with the evaluation. The basic steps of this approach include: (a) identifying or developing measures of the expected outcomes, (b) creating an appropriate research design that answers the question posed, (c) collecting and analyzing data, and (d) evaluating the object in light of the data and making recommendations. This approach can best be described as quantitative educational research.

Evaluations using an outcomes approach have to be individually tailored to meet the unique needs of each program. Individualized evaluation is necessary because gifted programs differ. The sets of objectives used to define each program element are not the same, and decision makers differ in their criteria for measuring program outcomes. Consequently, it is impossible to prescribe any one approach or method for evaluating program elements through an outcomes approach. To illustrate the outcome-oriented approach we will apply the process to portions of two program elements. The approach will be applied first to identification procedures and then to the curriculum.

One anticipated outcome of identification procedures may be to "discriminate between children who profit from a differentiated curriculum (i.e., gifted program) and those who do not." Thus, the effectiveness of identification procedures, criteria, and cutoffs can be assessed quantitatively, much in the same way as Pegnato and Birch (1959) demonstrated years ago.

In their study of junior high children, Pegnato and Birch determined how well various selection criteria and cutoffs (i.e., achievement test scores teacher nominations, group IQ scores, etc.) identified gifted children. Their procedure was to compare the composition of each group selected by a screening method with the gifted children group, those scoring an IQ of 136 or higher on the Stanford-Binet.

Each screening method was evaluated in terms of its effectiveness and efficiency. Effectiveness was defined as the extent to which a screening device identified all gifted children within a population. For example, if there are 100 gifted children in a population and a method identified 40, then its effectiveness rating is 40%. Efficiency was defined as the proportion of gifted children among those referred by a method. If 10 children are referred by a method and 8 are found to be gifted, the efficiency rating is 80%. Note that effectiveness ratings are not influenced by false positives (i.e., saying someone is gifted when he is not), but efficiency ratings are.

Although the techniques used by Pegnato and Birch may be too simplistic for today's conception of giftedness, paradigms can be derived from their work to evaluate today's identification procedures. One possibility is to utilize a prediction equation using success in a gifted program as the criterion variable and the identification criteria as independent variables. Thus, one would have an equation similar to this one: $Y' = b_0 + b^1 X_1 + b_2 X_2 \ldots + b_m X_m$ (Glass & Stanley, 1970, pp. 186–191), where Y is the criterion variable and X_n represents the dependent variables.

There are two major problems with this approach. The first is that giftedness is a multiple concept, so it would be necessary to have separate equations for different types of giftedness, i.e., general intellectual ability, creativity, etc. The second problem is defining and measuring success in the gifted program. Again, it would be necessary to have separate criteria for success for different types of giftedness.

In addition, it will be difficult to develop measures of program success regarded by individuals as being relevant and reliable. Although a difficult task, program evaluators must begin to assess identification criteria in terms of their predictive validity, i.e., how well students selected for a G/T program actually perform. Otherwise, we will not know whether criteria systematically fail to select children who would profit from a G/T program or, rather, select children who do poorly in the program. A good example of this approach may be found in an article by Reis and Renzulli (1982) and a study recently completed by the authors (Carter & Hamilton, 1984).

The curriculum is another area that can be evaluated through an outcomes approach. When curriculum objectives are specified, the effectiveness of the curriculum can be judged on student performance, i.e., what this student can do now that he was unable to do before the program. These student outcomes may be measured by the results of objective tests designed to measure the curriculum, student products (Reis & Renzulli, 1982), or behavior checklists, to name a few. For example, objectives, such as the ones listed in Table 3, imply specific outcomes as a result of participation in a gifted program. Objective tests, behavioral observations, and attitude inventories can be used to measure these outcomes. Appropriate research designs can be employed to answer important questions about this curriculum. One such question is, "Do the gifted meet the objective as a result of the curriculum?" This question demands that the evaluator compare gifted children who have completed the curriculum to gifted children who have not yet been exposed. This comparison is necessary to eliminate the possibility that gifted children, because they know they are gifted, may do reading and research on their own, obtaining the desired outcomes of the curriculum without ever formally going through it. If this proves to be the case, the curriculum is redundant and unnecessary.

It must be demonstrable that the curricula in gifted programs are different from those of the regular classroom. A differentiated curriculum may be characterized by any one or all of the following traits: the content is not offered in the regular classroom, material is presented in a much shorter time than in the regular classroom (curriculum compacting, Renzulli, Smith, & Reis, 1982), or material is presented in more depth or at a higher level of understanding than would occur in the regular classroom. Note that the first trait listed above can be evaluated qualitatively by comparing the objectives of the gifted curriculum with that of the regular classroom. However, the last two traits must be assessed quantitatively, in terms of outcomes. Therefore, it is necessary to design a study that compares the performance of the gifted to children from the regular classroom on measures of curriculum outcomes. Both groups would have to go through the same curriculum in the same manner. Data would be collected on their performance and compared. If the curriculum is truly differentiated, one would expect the gifted to out-perform the regular classroom students on the dependent measure.

We have used identification procedures and the curriculum as examples to highlight an outcomes-oriented approach to evaluation. There are many other objects that can be evaluated through the outcomes approach, but space limitations preclude their being described herein. All that is necessary to utilize this approach is that the object must include an objective that specifies an outcome. Then it becomes possible to identify or develop dependent measures to assess the outcome and create a research design that will answer the question the decision maker asks. We strongly encourage the use of the outcomes approach because only then will evaluators be able to determine whether a program is doing what it claims.

Before evaluators conduct an outcomes-oriented evaluation, they must become knowledgeable regarding certain evaluation issues specifically applicable to gifted populations. Two of the most critical ones are the appropriate measurement of educational outcomes and the selection of an appropriate control group. Space limitations prevent us from describing these issues here. However, the interested reader can find excellent information about these and other issues in articles by Ganopole (1982), Payne and Brown (1982), and Callahan (1983).

SUMMARY

The authors strongly advocate a program evaluation model that utilizes a process-oriented, content analysis approach, coupled with an outcome-oriented/quantitative design. The process-oriented approach will assess existing program content and analyze input factors which may influence program quality. Essentially, this type of approach investigates previous efforts in program planning, implementation, and evaluation. The outcome-oriented/quantitative approach determines whether the above-mentioned program elements achieved their anticipated outcomes. This involves a quantitative educational research design. This methodology (i.e., process-oriented content analysis and outcome-oriented/quantitative approach) should produce formative information for continuous program improvement.

In this age of accountability, it is no longer sufficient to subjectively determine that gifted and talented programs should continue to exist. Objective evidence must be provided that documents student and program growth as a result of differentiated educational experience based on precise organization, planning, implementation, and evaluation.

REFERENCES

Action for excellence. (1983). Denver, CO: Education Commission of the United States. Task Force on Education for Economic Growth.

Bard, W. R., & Gall, M. D. (1983). *Educational research: An introduction* (4th ed.). New York: Longman.

Bloom, B. S., Madeaus, G. F., & Hastings, J. T. (1981). *Evaluation to improve learning.* New York: McGraw Hill.

Bower, G. H., & Hilgard, E. R. (1981). *Theories of learning* (5th ed.). Englewood Cliffs, NJ: Prentice-Hall.

Boyer, E. L. (1983). *High school: A report on secondary education in America.* New York: Harper.

Callahan, C. M. (1983). Issues in evaluating programs for the gifted. *Gifted Child Quarterly, 27*(1), 3–7.

Campbell, D. T., & Stanley, J. C. (1963). *Experimental and quasi-experimental designs for research.* Chicago: Rand McNally.

Carter, K. R., & Hamilton, W. (1983). *Program evaluation report. Gifted and talented education, grades 3–5.* Greeley, CO: School District 6.

Carter, K. R., & Hamilton, W. (1984). *An evaluation study of curriculum units on higher level thinking skills and independent learning.* Greeley, CO: School District 6.

Cronbach, L. J. (1982). *Designing evaluations of educational and social programs.* San Francisco: Jossey-Bass.

Education and economic progress. (1983). Toward a National Education Policy. New York: The Carnegie Corporation.

Fox, L. H. (1979). Programs for the gifted and talented: An overview. In A.H. Passow (Ed.), *The gifted and talented: Their education and development.* The seventy-eighth yearbook of the National Society for the Study of Education (pp. 104–126). Chicago: University of Chicago Press.

Gallagher, J. J. (1975). *Teaching the gifted child* (2nd ed.). Boston: Allyn & Bacon.

Gallagher, J. J. (1979a). Research needs for the education of the gifted. In *Issues in gifted education.* Ventura, CA: National/State Leadership Training Institute on the Gifted and Talented.

Gallagher, J. J. (1979b). Issues in education for the gifted. In A. H. Passow (Ed.), *The gifted and talented: Their education and development.* The seventy-eighth yearbook of the National Society for the Study of Education (pp. 28–44). Chicago: University of Chicago Press.

Gallagher, J. J. (1981, November). *A report on the national survey.* Paper presented at the National Association for Gifted Children, Portland, OR.

Ganopole, S. J. (1982). Measuring the educational outcomes of gifted programs. *Roeper Review, 5*(1), 4–7.

Glass, G. V., & Stanley, J. C. (1970). *Statistical methods in education and psychology.* Englewood Cliffs, NJ: Prentice-Hall.

Marland, S. P. (1972). *Education of the gifted and talented* (Vol. 1). Report to the Congress of the United States by the U.S. Commissioner of Education. Washington, DC: U.S. Government Printing Office.

A nation at risk. (1983). (Stock No. 065-000-00177-2). Washington, DC: U.S. Government Printing Office.

Mitchell, B. M. (1984, February). An update on gifted/talented education in the U.S. *Roeper Review,* 161–163.

Nevo, D. (1983). The conceptualization of educational evaluation: An analytical review of the literature. *Review of Educational Research, 53*(1), 117–128.

Payne, D. A., & Brown, C. L. (1982). The use and abuse of control groups in program evaluation. *Roeper Review, 5*(1), 11–14.

Pegnato, C. W., & Birch, J. W. (1959). Locating gifted children in junior high schools: A comparison of methods. *Exceptional Children, 25*(7), 300–304.

Reis, S. M., & Renzulli, J. S. (1982). A research report on the revolving door identification model: A case for the broadened conception of giftedness. *Phi Delta Kappan, 63,* 619–620.

Renzulli, J. S. (1978). What makes giftedness? Reexamining a definition. *Phi Delta Kappan, 60,* 180–184.

Renzulli, J. S., Smith, L. H., & Reis, S. M. (1982, January). Curriculum compacting: An essential strategy for working with gifted children. *Elementary School Journal,* 185–194.

Rubenzer, R. L., & Twaite, J. A. (1979). Attitudes of 1,200 educators toward the education of the gifted and talented: Implications for teacher preparation. *Journal for the Education of the Gifted, 2*(4), 202–13.

Scriven, M. (1966). Student values as educational objectives. *Proceedings of the 1965 Invitational Conference on Testing Problems.* Princeton, NJ: Educational Testing Service.

Scriven, M. (1967). The methodology of evaluation. In R. E. Stake and Others (Eds.), *Perspectives on curriculum evaluation* (pp. 39–83). AERA Monograph Series on Curriculum Evaluation, No. 1. Chicago: Rand McNally.

3

The Role of Evaluation in Inservice and Staff Development for Educators of the Gifted

Marilynn J. Kulieke

Northwestern University

The use of evaluation in inservice training and staff development programs is too often limited in scope. This article expands the role of evaluation in gifted program inservice and staff development by providing evaluation techniques that have been used to determine the impact of inservice programs on teachers of the gifted.

Because a relationship between inservice training for teachers of the gifted and a better education for gifted students is generally assumed, the teacher

Editor's Note: From Kulieke, M. J. (1986). The role of evaluation in inservice and staff development for educators of the gifted. *Gifted Child Quarterly, 30*(3), 140-144. © 1986 National Association for Gifted Children. Reprinted with permission.

inservice training model has been adopted as a means of improving the education of gifted students. There is a need to investigate the validity of this relationship by systematically determining the kinds of inservice programs that have the greatest effect on behavioral and affective changes in teachers and students. Impact evaluation, or gauging the extent to which a program causes change in a desired direction, is a means of assessing program effect. Impact evaluation can help program planners make better decisions about the types of teacher inservice programs that are most valuable. Evaluation strategies can also be used in the initial stages of inservice development, to prioritize those areas that need most improvement. The following sections discuss the use of evaluation for inservice programs, the relationship between the type of inservice program and the type of evaluation, and suggest some general strategies for evaluating the impact of inservice programs.

SYSTEMATIC EVALUATION OF NEEDS

Evaluation can be used in the initial stages of inservice development by conducting a needs assessment. Rossi et al. (1979) define needs assessment as "the systematic appraisal of type, depth, and scope of problems as perceived by study targets or their advocates" (p. 82). In developing an inservice program, it is important to determine the extent to which teachers are experiencing difficulties teaching gifted students. This will permit the development of an inservice program that addresses and prioritizes those areas where teachers need most training. This strategy will increase the likelihood that the inservice program can affect teachers as well as the students.

A needs assessment can be accomplished in several different ways. It can be done formally or informally by written questionnaire or interview. However, it is important that it be done systematically. Informal polling of only a few teachers is inadequate to understand the true scope of the problems surrounding the education of gifted students in any school. It is often helpful to examine the opinions of several groups of individuals. Teachers of the gifted, regular classroom teachers, parents, students, school board members, and administrators all are groups that have important perspectives on how teachers can improve the education of gifted students. Each of these groups can be asked for opinions. To the extent that the various groups identify similar problems, it is likely that some major concerns have been identified.

A written questionnaire is one approach to collecting needs assessment information. Questionnaires are helpful in providing succinct measures of respondents' viewpoints. The disadvantages of questionnaires center around the constraints of using written forms of communication and the bias that can result from individual perceptions. Figure 1 is an example of one questionnaire that can be used. It should be noted that no closed questions are used on the questionnaire which might bias the dimensions along which the respondent is asked to focus.

Figure 1   Gifted Education Needs Assessment Questionnaire

Name (optional) _____

Are you a: (check one)?

☐ Teacher (Gifted Program)
☐ Teacher (Non-Gifted Program)
☐ Administrator
☐ Parent
☐ Student
☐ Board Member
☐ Other _____
                                                                (please specify)

1. What do you think is the greatest problem in educating gifted students at your school? (Please leave blank if you do not think that there are any problems.)

2. What do you think is the second greatest problem in educating gifted students at your school? (Please leave blank if you do not think that there are any problems.)

3. What do you think is the third greatest problem in educating gifted students at your school? (Please leave blank if you do not think that there are any problems.)

When completed questionnaires are returned, the magnitude of each problem cited can be determined by compiling responses and ranking them in order of the number making each response. In addition, the responses can be broken down by type of respondent (e.g., board member, parent, teacher). These group rankings can be compared and decisions made about prioritizing the needs ascertained from each group.

A more informal needs assessment approach can be done in a face-to-face interview. Interviews are advantageous in that they allow ideas to be expanded by using an interactive mode. This process allows ideas to surface that might otherwise be left out of an evaluation. The disadvantages of interviews include being difficult to analyze in quantitative ways and somewhat time-consuming as well. Also, the role of the interviewer is key to the kind of information that comes from the interview. The extensive research literature on this topic warrants perusal before the interview technique is selected. (Denzin, 1970; Richardson, Pohrenwend, Snell, & Klein, 1965; Kahn, & Cannell, 1957; Henerson, Morris, & Fitz-Gibbon, 1978).

It is important to choose individuals who will be interviewed or administered questionnaires by using a specific selection system. If time and money constraints dictate that an entire group (e.g., all parents of gifted students) will not be asked for feedback, it is important to sample randomly from the universe of those eligible to provide opinions. This type of sampling will help ensure that there is minimal bias.

In addition to information obtained from various groups on perceived needs, other methods can be used for determining areas upon which inservice training should focus. One of these is teacher observation. Morris and Fitz-Gibbon (1978) state that observational procedures call for someone to devote complete attention to the behavior of another individual or group within a natural setting and for a prescribed time period. Observations are advantageous because they provide a different conception of how a classroom is functioning. Often, what is perceived by others as occurring is not really happening at all. The disadvantages of observations are that they are time-consuming and costly to undertake. Observations also may not be representative of classroom happenings due to the presence of the observer. This can bias the information.

A systematic classroom observation effort provides useful information upon which to base inservice programming efforts. Peers, administrators, or experts in gifted education can observe classes of teachers in order to ascertain areas in which teachers are least proficient. A structured observation instrument provides quantitative information upon which to rank different areas of strength and weakness. An adaptation of the *Martinson-Weiner Rating Scale of Behaviors in Teachers of the Gifted* (Martinson, 1976) is shown in Figure 2. The Martinson-Weiner Rating Scale identifies and quantifies the existence of teaching behaviors that are important in teaching the gifted. This adaptation is scaled to make more consistent comparisons between each aspect of the classroom being observed. This approach has been used successfully to identify those areas of teacher weakness which can be addressed in inservice training programs.

A needs assessment can aid in developing a plan for gifted program inservice training that addresses weaknesses in the education of gifted students. Tailoring the inservice program to perceived weaknesses and weaknesses ascertained through classroom observation information can have powerful effects on the improvement of teaching and programs for the gifted.

INSERVICE TRAINING COMPONENTS AND EVALUATION

Inservice training components and impact evaluation are inextricably bound to each other. The type of program will to a large extent determine the kind of impact assessment that can be undertaken. Evaluation research points out the strong relationship of treatment (i.e., the inservice training program) and outcomes that can be expected from any such program. The length, the quality, and the topic of the program are major determinants of the kind of evaluation that would be optimal.

Figure 2   Observation Form for Use with Teachers of the Gifted*

Directions:

Taking into account the content of this class, how proficient do you feel the teacher is at using each of the following teaching strategies? It is recommended that teachers be observed for *two* 30-minute periods before and after relevant inservice work, using this form as a guide.

Conducts Group Discussions	Excellent	Good	Fair	Poor	Very Poor
Teacher withholds own ideas and conclusions.	5	4	3	2	1
Teacher encourages participation of students in discussions.	5	4	3	2	1
Teacher poses interpretive questions for students.	5	4	3	2	1
Selects Questions That Stimulate Higher-Level Thinking					
Students evaluate situations, problems, issues.	5	4	3	2	1
Students ask analytic questions.	5	4	3	2	1
Students generalize from concrete to abstract at advanced levels.	5	4	3	2	1
Uses Varied Teaching Strategies Effectively					
Teacher is sensitive to students' responses.	5	4	3	2	1
Teacher maintains a balance between active and passive activities.	5	4	3	2	1
Teacher deliberately shifts teaching strategies with students.	5	4	3	2	1
Utilizes Critical Thinking Skills in Appropriate Contexts					
Teacher utilizes inductive and deductive reasoning and is able to apply techniques in classroom.	5	4	3	2	1
Teacher encourages student development of inference and evaluation of argument skills.	5	4	3	2	1
Teacher encourages analogical thinking.	5	4	3	2	1
Encourages Independent Thinking and Open Inquiry					
Students compare and contrast different issues, using objective evidence.	5	4	3	2	1
Students engage in lively debate of controversial issues.	5	4	3	2	1
Students and teacher reflect an open/challenging attitude toward knowledge.	5	4	3	2	1
Understands and Encourages Student Ideas and Student-Directed Work					
Teacher encourages students to try new approaches.	5	4	3	2	1
Teacher is tolerant to students' attempts to find solutions to problems.	5	4	3	2	1
Teacher encourages "guesses" by students and facilitates evaluation of guesses by students.	5	4	3	2	1
Teacher helps students to realize that research involves trial and error.	5	4	3	2	1
Demonstrates Understanding of the Educational Implications of Giftedness					
Teacher uses implications of characteristics in the classroom operation, selection of materials, schedules, and questions.	5	4	3	2	1
Teacher uses management procedures that maximize individual differences of students in the learning process.	5	4	3	2	1
Teacher uses advanced organizers for instruction and organizes curriculum around the highest level skill, concept, or idea that a group of gifted learners can master.	5	4	3	2	1

*Adapted from *Martinson-Weiner Rating Scale of Behaviors in Teachers of the Gifted* (Martinson, 1976).

The *length* of the inservice program is one element to be considered in making a decision about the type of evaluation plan to be developed. A two-hour inservice would probably provide a weak program upon which to develop an elaborate evaluation plan. Using less complex means of evaluation would be best for assessing a program that takes place over a short time span.

The *quality* of a program is another important aspect of determining the type of evaluation necessary. After the needs for inservice training are determined, a well-defined, relevant program should be located or developed that can address those needs. Two major evaluation concerns relate to quality of the inservice program. The first is how well the planned inservice training program relates to the identified needs. To the extent that the program matches those needs and has the potential for meeting those needs, the evaluation can provide relatively useful information. This concern emphasizes the importance of having a well-defined inservice program in advance of determining an evaluation plan. If, after examining the planned program, it is felt that the program is not addressing the identified needs, an evaluation of anticipated impacts will not be successful.

A second concern related to the quality of the program is the degree to which the program was implemented as planned. No matter what a program looks like on paper, it can change substantially in presentation. For this reason it is necessary to monitor the implementation of the inservice program to determine the extent to which the implementation could have an influence on teacher outcomes.

The *kind* of inservice program may also influence the type of evaluation that can be carried out. It is much easier to assess the impact of a program on cognitive behaviors than on affective outcomes. For example, a program which has a goal of training teachers to write student objectives for gifted classes would be easier to assess than a program which has a goal of helping students cope with their giftedness. The type of evaluation plan would be quite different depending upon the goal of the inservice program.

In determining the type of evaluation plan that would be optimal for an inservice training program, it is important to examine each of these relationships (length, quality, and kind) between program and evaluation. This will aid the development of an evaluation plan well-matched to needs.

EVALUATION STRATEGIES FOR INSERVICE TRAINING OF GIFTED PROGRAM TEACHERS

Determining the impact of any educational program is a difficult endeavor. The following are several evaluation strategies that are helpful in assessing the impact of participation in an inservice program. The strategy to be chosen depends on the existence and degree to which the concerns discussed previously are factors. To the exent that any of them poses a major problem, a less time-consuming and sophisticated strategy to assess impact is warranted. Time might be better spent planning and developing a program which offers greater opportunity for producing change.

In examining changes in behaviors or attitudes, it is important to determine a baseline from which change can be inferred. There are three commonly used strategies to assess change. The first is to measure an individual before the inservice begins and at one or more points after the inservice took place. The second is to find a comparison group of individuals who are similar to the participants of the inservice, but who did not participate in the inservice sessions, and to measure both groups before and at one or more points after the inservice. These designs are forms of quasi-experimental research (Cook & Campbell, 1979). A third strategy for examining change, which is less time-consuming and less reliable, is to use the individual as the baseline, and use a questionnaire or interview to determine the kinds of changes that occurred as a result of participation in the inservice program.

As an example of these techniques for assessing long-term effects of inservice, consider the staff development inservice program which has a goal of helping teachers of gifted to develop instructional techniques tailored to learning styles of the gifted. The inservice is presented during a teacher inservice day and all teachers of gifted students in a particular school participate in the inservice session. In order to assess change using a comparison group model, it is necessary to find another group of teachers of the gifted who are not receiving this training. Another school might collaborate in these efforts by providing teachers who consent to be tested.

When a group receiving the treatment and a comparison group are identified, an instrument must be developed or located which is tailored to the behaviors that are expected to be changed as a result of participation in the inservice program. Measurement centering around teachers' current instructional techniques provides an assessment of inservice effect. Selection of an observation measure such as the adapted Martinson-Weiner Scale (see Figure 2) would include observing the classrooms of both teachers participating in the inservice and teachers in the comparison group. The groups can be observed in advance of the inservice and then again a short time after the inservice. To the extent that changes in teachers' behaviors are observed for inservice participants but not for nonparticipants, effects can be better attributed to the inservice program. If a comparison group is not available, one must forego this model and use a pre/post evaluation of change or an individual retrospective change evaluation.

The technique of using pretest and posttest observation only for inservice participants provides less clear data about changed instructional techniques. A possibility exists that other factors contributed to the change. One way to minimize such possible effects is to ask inservice participants to rate the extent to which they feel the inservice is responsible for any changes in their instructional techniques.

The retrospective change evaluation is easiest to implement. It consists of a questionnaire or interview that asks the teachers about any effects the program had upon them. The existence of change is based on the perceptions of the

Figure 3   Sample Posttest Only Impact Questions

To what extent do you feel that the inservice program entitled "Instructional Strategies for Teachers of the Gifted" has increased the frequency with which you do each of the following?

	Very much more often since the inservice	More often since the inservice	A little more often since the inservice	No more often since the inservice
I withhold my own ideas and conclusions.	4	3	2	1
I encourage participation of students and discussions.	4	3	2	1
I pose interpretive questions for students.	4	3	2	1

teacher about those effects. Some sample questions for examining teacher instructional techniques are shown in Figure 3. This is the most common form of impact evaluation for inservice program. It is not costly and is relatively easy to administer.

CONCLUSIONS

Evaluation strategies can be used at different stages of the teacher inservice process. At the preliminary planning stages, evaluation strategies can be used to help determine the content for the inservice training program. If an inservice program is a substantive program which would merit the use of better evaluation strategies, quasi-experimental research designs can be used to provide a better assessment of inservice training impacts. Pretests, as well as one or more posttests with those participating in the inservice program and with a comparison group, can be helpful strategies for determining actual inservice program impacts.

The evaluation of inservice programs provides a challenge to those who undertake them. The potential of inservice programs for helping gifted students makes them a valuable component of the educational process. The development of inservice programs that are well-defined and worthy of systematic evaluation is a first step. Using evaluation strategies that provide good information about inservice training impact is the next step. Together these can make an important contribution to the education of gifted students.

REFERENCES

Cook, T. D. & Campbell, D. T. (1979). *Quasi-experimentation: Design and analysis issues for field settings.* Chicago, IL: Rand McNally.

Denzin, N. K. (1970). *The research act.* Chicago, IL: Adline Publishing Company.

Henerson, M. E., Morris, L. L., & Fitz-Gibbon, C. T. (1978). *How to measure attitudes.* Beverly Hills, CA: Sage Publications.

Kahn, R. L. and Cannel, C. F. (1957). *The dynamics of interviewing: Theory, technique, and cases.* New York, NY: John Wiley.

Martinson, R. A. (1976). *A guide toward better teaching for the gifted.* Ventura, CA: Office of the Ventura County Superintendent of Schools.

Morris, L. L. & Fitz-Gibbon, C. T. (1978). *How to measure attitudes.* Beverly Hills, CA: Sage Publications.

Rossi, P. H., Freeman, H. E., & Wright, S. R. (1979). *Evaluation: A systematic approach.* Beverly Hills, CA: Sage Publications.

4

Anchoring Assessment With Exemplars: Why Students and Teachers Need Models

Grant Wiggins

Center on Learning, Assessment, and School Structure

This essay presents an argument for the use of examples that set a clear standard for student performance. As educators implement new forms of assessments, they should calibrate local standards to exemplars, anchoring the highest point of their scoring system to examples of excellent performance. Educators should not be fearful of describing superlative performance even though all students may not reach those expert levels. Four types of performance criteria are suggested: impact, process, form and content. Examples of assessment initiatives grounded in models of excellent performance are also summarized.

Editor's Note: From Wiggins, G. (1996). Anchoring assessment with exemplars: Why students and teachers need models. *Gifted Child Quarterly, 40*(2), 66-69. © 1996 National Association for Gifted Children. Reprinted with permission.

The J. Peterman clothing catalogue had been coming to our house for a few years before I began to read it with any care. One day though, as I was leafing through it upon its arrival, I was struck by a particularly wonderful write-up for a fairly ordinary product:

Listening to Big Yellow

Hobsbawn (not his real name) no longer plunges into deep depression when he flips on the Weather Channel. Betty, once incapacitated by feelings of vulnerability, now seeks out the most challenging muck. Harry, once angry and irritable, feared he'd "go berserk" at work some April morning. Now he has a smile for everyone. What does it mean when vulcanized rubber can alter what we think of as personality? Should we question our concept of the sell?

Big Yellow. Galoshes with the fortitude of a Caterpillar tractor and the cheerfulness of a school bus. Just below-the-knee length. Slip them on over shoes or boots (there's lots of room to tuck in your pants), then cinch tight. Cotton jersey lining. Heavy-duty tread. Totally and absolutely waterproof. Wearing them through rain, snow, slush, mud, mire, and muck is like eating a bowl of McCann's oatmeal topped with butter churned from your own cow's milk.

This is wonderful writing: vivid, rich, and as seemingly persuasive as ad copy can be. From that point on, I made it a point to read each issue thoroughly—not because I wish to buy the items but because I am always on the lookout for similar "exemplars" examples of performance that set a clear standard.

My aim in this brief essay is to sing the praises of such exemplars not merely as illustrative and engaging aids in teaching but as anchors for an assessment system, particularly one geared to gifted and talented students. For unless students are constantly exposed to the best possible products, performances, and specifications in each field, they will never produce the best work that they are capable of producing. And they will also be educationally deprived: ignorant of the kinds and quality of work expected of talented people in the professional workplace.

What do I mean by "anchors"? Anchors are the samples of work that set the standard for the highest as well as every other level of performance in an assessment. We are most familiar with the idea of anchors for scoring scales in writing assessments (especially through the Advanced Placement Essays and state-wide writing tests), but they exist in many fields, including music, foreign language, and speech.

What I am proposing is that faculties should always calibrate their local standards to such exemplars, anchoring the highest point on their scoring system with such examples of excellent performance. This is the only way for teachers as well as students to have valid, compelling, and stable targets at which to aim.

Invariably people react cautiously to such a proposal. While they accept in principle the idea that models are valuable and that performance standards should be valid, clear, and educative, they often balk at using such models to anchor assessment. They often express the fear that students who have their works compared to the works of the most proficient will be rendered depressed and insecure by such comparisons.

Putting the Research to Use

The arguments advanced in this essay suggest at least two practical implications for educators. The first is that the standards for student performance should account for the full range of possible performances, including those which exemplify the best work possible. The second is that students need to be exposed to many such genuine models and subsequently provided with the kind of feedback which helps them improve their performance.

Such a fear is misplaced. Critics of the idea are typically confusing "expectations" with "standards." Expectations involve what we assume many students can and should be able to meet with good instruction and pupil effort. A standard, however; is something different. It represents the best work possible; a standard is a standard whether or not *anyone* in the school can meet it. Big Yellow sets a standard for descriptive writing even if no students can (yet) write that well. We don't expect students to get the highest possible score anymore than we expect a high school runner to clock a sub-four-minute mile. On the other hand, we don't hide world-class times from athletes—and for good reason.

The point in anchoring an assessment system by exemplars is to set worthy and educative goals. The purpose of a student assessment system is to *improve* performance, not just audit it. Tests do not merely measure, they teach; assessments should instruct students and faculty alike about what outstanding work is. We should thus ensure that our assessment tasks are exemplary, not just out performance standards: that's a crucial part of the argument for "authentic assessment." Assessment is then educative; instruction must naturally involve the study and emulation of exemplars.

All performers need models; in other words, that's how all performers improve. It's also how people are inspired to improve. No musician, athlete, or graphic artist would find this idea of standard-referenced assessment fearful as a consequence. On the contrary, we are doomed to endless mucking around or mere good faith efforts based on a limited conception of the possible if we are deprived of genuine models of performance. Gifts and talents only take you so far; you need always to discover that a great deal more is possible and that study of the great is desirable.

By contrast, to live in an educational world absent of true models (as almost all students do) helps explain our failure to raise national academic performance significantly over time in comparison with the arts, athletics, and areas such as debate and speech. Secure tests and "guess what I am looking for" approaches to test preparation may keep students more anxious but it won't improve performance. We can demand much higher levels of performance if there are no secrets or mysteries about what quality products and performances look like.

In a world of secrecy and teacher fatalism about what is possible in terms of performance gains, we then flinch from being a standard-referenced system and revert to being a norm-referenced system in the strict sense, i.e. anchoring our assessment by what is now the norm. This is a strategy that fails to raise standards and expectations—the goal is not to build a system out of what *is*, but of what *ought* to be. In fact, progress is only possible by a system that assumes performers should work to *overcome* best performance instead of assuming its impossibility (as too many educators do) and where models are constantly studied and which serve as points of reference in assessment.

A second fear is that anchoring instruction and assessment with models can only inhibit genuine creative talent. This is a particularly strong fear among some teachers of gifted and talented students. While the fear is understandable, it is important to note that the operant word here is "models"—the plural. The easiest way to teach students more effectively without inhibiting their creativity is to purvey multiple, diverse models of excellence. Let them read Austen and Joyce as well as Peterman's catalogue to master description; let them hear the speeches of Desmond Tutu, Ronald Reagan, Jesse Jackson, and Barbara Jordan; let them learn from Stephen Jay Gould, John McPhee, Lewis Thomas, and Oliver Sacks on how to describe phenomena and make findings of interest to the reader.

Even with diverse models, however, creativity can be hampered by the wrong scoring criteria and scoring rubrics built upon them. Real performance and all enterprising behavior is about causing a desired impact. Too much school testing, however, relies on criteria concerning orthodox content, formats or procedures. You must write up labs a certain way; you must use a five-step proof in geometry; you must write a five-paragraph essay, etc. Such assessments typically do not care whether the write-ups are powerful or persuasive, merely that they are correct in content and procedure.

It is vital, however, that we learn to better assess the question at the heart of performance: Did the performance work? Was the purpose achieved, even if in an unorthodox manner? Creativity can only be evoked and developed if we assess primarily for impact as opposed to content, process and format only. That's why we at the Center on Learning, Assessment, and School Structure (CLASS) work with teacher-designers to better emphasize impact criteria in their assessments. Figure 1 gives examples of such criteria, in contrast with the other three types.

Figure 1   Four Types of Performance Criteria With Examples

Impact	Process	Form	Content
Effective • Client Satisfied • Problem Solved • Audience Moved • Situation Settled • Healthful • Persuasive	**Purposeful** • Efficient • Adaptive • Self-Regulated • Persistent • Enterprising • (Self-)Critical	**Well Designed** • Fit (form follows function) • Authentic • Elegant • Clever	**Accurate** • Correct • Informed • Valid • Verified • Justified • Rigorous
High Quality • Tops in its Class • Offers Value • Competitive • Ethical • Novel • Unusual	**Thoughtful** • Considerate • Responsive • Inquisitive • Methodical, Logical • Critical • Inclusive	**Well Crafted** • Organized • Thorough • Precise • Mechanically Sound • Clear • Concise	**Apt** • Focused • Required • Client-sought
	Skilled linked to task- and situation-specific skills: e.g., well written, argued, discussed, reasons, drawn, etc.)	**Style** • Voice (authentic) • Graceful	**Sophisticated** • Deep • Insightful • Powerful • Expert • Justified

Process, form, and content matter: But while they are necessary to performance, they are not sufficient. The point is never to merely emulate the surface or mechanical traits of performances and performers, but their effect, their ability to persuade an audience, satisfy a client request, or solve a problem. Otherwise we *do* stifle performance creativity. Thus, many state writing assessments *do* run the risk of undercutting good writing if they score for focus, organization, style, and mechanics—even to high standards—without once asking judges to consider whether the writing is powerful, memorable, provocative, or moving (all impact-related criteria).

"But that's so subjective!" Really? It's in fact quite objective; one can find out empirically if the work moves or provokes. In fact, such criteria are more objective than traits like "focus" or "organization" about which English teachers can and do passionately disagree. More to the point, go back to the beginning of my essay. Isn't Big Yellow a memorable piece of description? I think so, and I don't think we will need to get into any ideological blood-baths over aesthetics, particularly if we use multiple samples judged to be excellent by experts in the field, as mentioned above.

When "impact" criteria are highlighted in assessment and "form" and "process" criteria are downplayed, we in fact open the door to greater creativity not less. Then, someone can and will find a new way to achieve a significant impact. Unless we highlight "impact" criteria, the student in fact has no real performance goal other than to please the teacher or mimic orthodox approaches. "Is this what you want, Mr. Smith?" is a vital sign of the failure to teach students that performance criteria are not about tastes or teacher preferences but about what actually tends to work in the wider world—i.e., achieve bona fide performance purposes.

A third concern about using exemplars is that even if there is commonsensical value in knowing what is possible, there is little practical value in anchoring assessment with true models if the gap between the possible and the actual is too vast. This would be a valid complaint if all I were recommending was the use of models. But an educative assessment system is one that builds in 1) descriptions of the *varieties* of quality in performance, *and* 2) student self-assessment and self-adjustment. Both are only possible if we *purvey a full range of possible performances,* along a scoring scale of significant size, with a succinct rubric to summarize the differences.

Improvement depends upon performer-friendly feedback. And that requires assessments which enable the performer to see incremental progress of a fairly small degree, and to verify where they are and have been. As the system of karate belts, rankings in chess, cross country racing times, computer game scoring, or weight reduction systems reveal so clearly, we need the *incentive,* not just the data, provided by on-going, small-change-sensitive feedback if we are to persist with challenging work.

Such a system is also the only way to avoid a practical problem afflicting many programs: the setting of standards that are too low because of the pervasive influence of the patterns of typical student performance. We may over-reward talented people for their talents; we are easily taken in by mere articulateness and cleverness as opposed to craftsmanship and effectiveness. A key reason is that we haven't taken the time to develop a standard-referenced assessment system to accommodate their higher-than-normal levels of performance. All state and national testing systems have too low a ceiling to adequately differentiate good from great work. And if the truth be told, too many teachers are unfamiliar with the highest levels of performance in many fields they teach to develop such a scoring system.

How might we begin to honor this idea of grounding our teaching and testing in models? How might teachers develop standard-referenced systems more effectively? Here are some ideas:

- Booklets are available from the Advanced Placement Exam containing samples of past essays in such subjects as English, History, and Biology. Why not anchor a local scoring system with them? And not merely in high school programs, but middle school programs.
- The Carleton School Board in Nepean, Ontario, has for many years published what they call Exemplar Booklets containing samples of a full range of student writing, with commentary. Every student, teacher, and parent in the system has a copy.

- The American Council on the Teaching of Foreign Languages has developed a rich set of materials containing rubrics and samples that span the full range from fluent to novice, in reading, writing, speaking, and listening.
- One teacher we at CLASS worked with anchored her first-grade audio-book-tape project with professional models. Analysis of the models by the students, with teacher coaching, yielded a list of criteria that the students ended up using in their own self-assessments.
- Heritage High School in Littleton, Colorado, builds its exit writing exam out of the entry-level exam at Colorado State University. The writing prompt, the rubric, and the anchor papers used in scoring all come from the Freshman Placement exam in writing.

As I noted above, we should be anchoring teacher work in assessment with models, too. Consider these examples of anchoring local test *design* with exemplars:

- The American Federation of Teachers (AFT) has published a set of materials with samples from exams from around the world in the core academic areas. (And AFT President Al Shanker has long sung the praises of Scout Merit Badge requirements for setting performance standards. Many Merit badges exist for such school-related subjects as American cultures, meteorology, and technology.)
- One can purchase all previous exams from the International Baccalaureate (IB) program without being a member. You can also purchase a booklet containing a sample of some of their best student research papers from around the world (an extended research project in the final year of school is an IB requirement).
- If you are a teacher at the middle or elementary level, get copies of all major tests and project requirements from teachers of advanced high school courses and samples of the range of student work
- Harvard University publishes all freshmen exams in the Lamont Library, and they are a treasure trove for designing essay questions. Despite the constant K-12 educator carping about college testing as a terrible model, many of the exams are first-rate: creative, challenging, and rarely prone to fishing for trivia. Here are three examples:

1. Your government decides it wants to harvest the rare and commercially important snail *Helix memoresus* for its memory-enhancing mucus. The government decides to adopt a fixed-quota harvesting policy.

As an expert naturalist, explain to the myopic politicians the potential problems of such a policy: What advice would you give about how to set the harvest and why?

2. Poetry Examination

As to twentieth century poetry . . . it will, I think, move against poppy-cock, it will be harder and saner, it will be . . . 'nearer the bone.' It will be as much like granite as it can be, its force will lie in its truth . . . I want it so, austere, direct, free from emotional slither:"

(Ezra Pound, 1912)

How has Pound's notion of modern poetry manifested itself in the modern poems we have read? Has his prediction come true?

3. You find that the *Glaucium flavum* has a population on Nantucket Island that is significantly larger than those on the Massachusetts mainland. You find the difference is due to growth rates. The difference in growth rate may be due to genetic differentiation or environmental differences.

Design a field experiment to arbitrate between these hypotheses.

The goal is to improve everyone's performance over time. That can occur only if we keep meeting our greatest challenge as educators: to show the students that they can be better while making it seem possible to be better than they are. That requires better models and better feedback than we now provide.

REFERENCES

Wiggins, G. (1993). *Assessing student performance: Exploring the purpose and limits of testing.* San Francisco: Jossey-Bass.

5

The Assessment of Creative Products in Programs for Gifted and Talented Students

Sally M. Reis

Joseph S. Renzulli

University of Connecticut

Formal evaluation of student products completed in programs for the gifted and talented seldom occurs. Few instruments exist for this purpose, and reliability and validity information is not often available for the instruments that do exist. In this article, the development of the *Student Product Assessment Form* is reviewed. A description of the results obtained from content validation procedures, reliability findings, scoring, and interrater agreement and reliability techniques are provided.

Editor's Note: From Reis, S. M., & Renzulli, J. S. (1991). The assessment of creative products in programs for gifted and talented students. *Gifted Child Quarterly, 35*(3), 128-134. © 1991 National Association for Gifted Children. Reprinted with permission.

"I would argue that the starting point, indeed the bedrock of all studies of creativity, is an analysis of creative products, a determination of what it is that makes them different from more mundane products."

Donald W. MacKinnon (1987, p. 120)

Donald MacKinnon, a noted researcher in the area of creativity, believes that the criterion by which other facets of creativity should be studied is the creative product (1987). According to MacKinnon, the different facets of creativity, which include the creative process, the creative person, and the creative solution, should be defined with reference to the creative product. MacKinnon defines creative processes as those resulting in creative products, creative persons as those who bring creative products into existence, and creative situations as a set of circumstances which permits, fosters, and makes possible creative productions.

Rhodes (1987) expressed similar views on creative products. According to Rhodes, products can present a record of one's thoughts at the moment a new concept is born, and since products are artifacts of thought, the analysis of products can help to reconstruct the mental process of inventing. Thus, investigation into the nature of the creative process can proceed from product to person and then to process and to press (the relationship between human beings and their environment).

The analysis of evaluation of creative products can provide insight into the creative potential of students who participate in gifted and talented programs. It may also provide input into the process which is used to complete products. How can we effectively and fairly evaluate products? How do we determine what it is that makes products creative and different? Amabile (1983) suggests that we must "somehow quantify our notions of what makes a creative product and specify objective means for assessing those qualities . . ." (p. 26). Because of the difficulties in making strictly objective assessments of creative products, she concludes that, "the assessment of creativity simply cannot be achieved by objective analysis alone. Some type of subjective assessment is required" (p. 27).

Getzels and Csikszentmihalyi (1976); Jackson and Messick (1965); and Sobel and Rothenberg (1980) have discussed the criteria by which products should be judged, agreeing that the major responsibility for assessing the creativity of a product is placed on the values and experience of the judge(s). Usually no specific guidelines are available to those doing the judging. Therefore, the reliability and validity of the judgments can be questioned. Little research has been conducted in the area of product evaluation in gifted and talented programs. This study describes the development of a product rating scale designed for this purpose.

EVALUATION OF CREATIVE PRODUCTS

A review of numerous instruments for product and process evaluation of completed student products in a gifted program reveals a paucity of research in this area. Few instruments are available for perusal, and even fewer have been evaluated in terms of reliability, validity, or field test data. Treffinger (1987, p. 114), an expert in creativity, identified 11 major areas of opportunity and concern in the area of creativity assessment, including the need for demonstration of reliability and validity of instruments for evaluating products based on creativity criteria. In a publication compiled by the Council for Exceptional Children (1979) entitled *Sample Instruments for the Evaluation of Programs for the Gifted and Talented,* seven different gifted programs from the United States provided detailed descriptions of their evaluation process. Only one program included product evaluation as one of the program objectives. Fifty gifted programs were contacted as a part of this study, and few used any formal evaluation of student products. Those that did evaluate products used a locally developed form on which students indicated what they had learned by completing their product. Teachers of the gifted indicated that their evaluation consisted of a verbal exchange with the student and that very often no written assessment of the student's product was filed in the student's record.

Putting the Research to Use

Many students are involved in gifted and talented programs in which they develop products. Evaluation of these products is often not completed or completed in an informal way. If the evaluation of student products were organized and conducted on a regular basis, a record could be kept of this important aspect of student work. The *Student Product Assessment Form (SPAF)* was developed to aid teachers in their evaluation of student products. It has been field tested for several years and has proven to be both valid and reliable. In districts where *SPAF* is used, a copy of the summary sheet (Figure 1) is included in the permanent record folder of each student who has competed a product that academic year. The accumulated summary sheets provide an overview of all products completed in the gifted program and provide an academic portfolio of a student's creative products.

More recently, product evaluation forms have been developed by Archambault and Gubbins (1980), Callahan (1980), Tuttle (1980), and Westberg (1990). All of these forms have been utilized in research and evaluation studies and will be involved in future field test situations. Tuttle's form was designed to provide a rater with a valid basis for assessing the quality of the work and the implementation of research and communication skills. According to Tuttle, this Product Evaluation Form proved to be a valid and reliable instrument to assess implementation of advanced research and communication skills when used by trained raters. Tuttle also noted that his form is appropriate only for certain types of products: those involving research skills and the sharing of the product with an audience.

Callahan's *Product Evaluation Form* (1980) was specifically designed to evaluate Type III investigations in a gifted program based on *The Enrichment Triad Model* (Renzulli, 1977). Callahan devised the form to determine whether or not the student had familiarized himself/herself with the problems, techniques, methodologies, environment, product, and audience of the interest area that s/he selected for the investigation. No distinction is made between process and product skills in either Tuttle's or Callahan's instruments.

Amabile (1983) advocated the use of a consensual technique for creativity assessment. The major features of the consensual assessment technique are as follows. The task being analyzed should lead to a product or observable response that can be assessed. The task should be open-ended to permit flexibility and novelty in responses, and the task should not be dependent upon certain special skills such as drawing ability or verbal fluency. The assessment procedure as described by Amabile includes five requirements. First, the judges should all have some experience with the domain being assessed. Implied in this requirement is that judges have enough familiarity with the domain to have developed, over a period of time, some implicit criteria for creativity, technical goodness, and so on. The second procedural requirement for the assessment procedure is that judges assess independently. Third, judges are asked to make assessments on other dimensions in addition to creativity. Judges are also instructed to rate the products relative to one another on the dimensions in question as opposed to, for example, the greatest works ever produced in that domain. Last, each judge should view products in a different random order and consider the dimensions being assessed in a different random order (Amabile, 1983, pp. 37–39). Amabile also recommends that each dimension of the instrument used to rate products be analyzed for interjudge reliability.

Westberg (1990) used Amabile's (1983) consensual assessment technique to develop an instrument for assessing the creative productivity of inventions made by elementary and middle school students. Judges regarded as experts in creative productivity used Westberg's *Invention Evaluation Instrument* to evaluate student inventions. A factor analysis of this instrument indicated that the 11 items loaded on 3 factors: originality, technical goodness, and aesthetic appeal. The interrater reliability for the instrument as a whole was 0.96.

Bessemer and Treffinger (1981) discovered similar results regarding the paucity of research in a review of the literature on the characteristics of creative products and subsequently developed *The Creative Product Analysis Matrix* (CPAM). The authors of CPAM proposed that groups of related attributes cluster along three different but interrelated dimensions: (a) novelty, (b) resolution, and (c) elaboration and synthesis. They define novelty as the degree of originality of the product in terms of new concepts, new processes, or new materials used. Resolution of a product reflects the degree to which a product resolves the problem implied by its creation, and elaboration and synthesis are described as the " . . . stylistic attributes of the product by focusing on aspects of complexity or elaboration of the product's conception, and the refinement, synthesis and elegance shown in its manifestation" (Bessemer & O'Quin, 1987, p. 342). Additional research was conducted on whether or not subjects would evaluate creative products in a manner consistent with the proposed model. Selecting a variety of creative products, a judging instrument based on CPAM and called the *CPAM Adjective Checklist* was developed which contained 110 adjectives and adjectival phrases describing the three dimensions of novelty, resolution, elaboration and synthesis. Based on this research, 12 subscales were constructed from the 110 different words. Under the dimension of novelty, 3 subscales emerged: original, germinal, and startling. Under the dimension of resolution, 2 subscales emerged: logical and useful. Under the dimension of elaboration and synthesis, 3 subscales emerged: elegant/organic, attractive, and well-crafted. Reliability and validity studies conducted on CPAM are reported by the authors as quite positive. The use of CPAM in the research studies reported in the literature (Bessemer & Treffinger, 1981; Bessemer & O'Quin, 1987) is extremely promising for the evaluation of the creative products of adults.

DEVELOPMENT OF THE STUDENT PRODUCT ASSESSMENT FORM

Content Validity

Description of the Student Product Assessment Form. The first stage in the development of the *Student Product Assessment Form (SPAF)* (Reis, 1981) was to outline the content around which the instrument was to be constructed. Toward this end, letters were sent to coordinators of 50 long-established gifted programs throughout the country. Program coordinators and teachers were asked to provide the researchers with any forms or instruments used to evaluate student products. Every response indicated that formal product evaluation rarely occurred; when it did, the instruments used were locally developed and lacked reliability and validity information. Most of the product rating forms were very brief and sketchy, consisting of questions students were asked to answer upon completion of a product, for example, what did you learn by doing this project?

A review of literature was also undertaken in an effort to identify methods of evaluating student products completed in gifted programs. As was pointed out earlier, a shortage of instruments designed for this purpose was found. Few of the instruments available were evaluated in terms of reliability, validity, or field test research. Additionally, all available forms and scales that were examined

Figure 1   Student Product Assessment Form Summary Sheet

Name(s) _____   Date _____

District _____   School _____

Teacher _____   Grade _____ Sex _____

Product (Title and/or Brief Description) _____
_____

Number of Months Student(s) worked on Product _____

FACTORS	RATING*	NOT APPLICABLE
1. Early Statement of Purpose	_____	_____
2. Problem Focusing	_____	_____
3. Level of Resources	_____	_____
4. Diversity of Resources	_____	_____
5. Appropriateness of Resources	_____	_____
6. Logic, Sequence, and Transition	_____	_____
7. Action Orientation	_____	_____
8. Audience	_____	_____
9. Overall Assessment	_____	_____
A. Originality of the Idea	_____	_____
B. Achieved Objectives Stated in Plan	_____	
C. Advanced Familiarity with Subject	_____	
D. Quality Beyond Age/Grade Level	_____	
E. Care, Attention to Detail, etc	_____	
F. Time, Effort, Energy	_____	
G. Original Contribution	_____	
Comments:	_____	
Person completing this form:	_____	

*Rating Scales: Factors 1–8

	Factors 9A - 9G	
5 - To a great extent	5 = Outstanding	2 = Below Average
3 - Somewhat	4 = Above Average	1 = Poor
1 - To a limited extent	3 = Average	

were either geared toward adult products (Bessemer & Treffinger, 1981); geared to specific products such as inventions (Westberg, 1990); or judged to be sketchy, inadequate, and incomplete for use in the evaluation of gifted students' products.

Based upon the examination of the literature and our years of familiarity with the outstanding products developed by gifted students, a new form was designed (see Summary Sheet for form in Figure 1) to provide raters with a valid and reliable basis for assessing the quality of products completed in gifted and talented programs. Fifteen items were generated which assess both individual aspects as well as the overall excellence of the product. Each item represents a single characteristic on which raters should focus their attention. Items 1 through 8 are divided into three related parts:

1. *The Key Concept.* This concept is always presented first and is printed in large type. It should serve to focus the rater's attention on the main idea or characteristic being evaluated.

2. *The Item Description.* Following the Key Concept are one or more descriptive statements about how the characteristic might be reflected in the student's product.

3. *Examples.* In order to help clarify the meaning of the items, an actual example of students' work is provided. These examples are intended to elaborate upon the meaning of both the Key Concept and the Item Description. The examples are presented in italics following each item description.

An example of item 4 is included below:

DIVERSITY OF RESOURCES

Has the student made an effort to use several different types of resource materials in the development of the product? Has the student used any of the following information sources in addition to the standard use of encyclopedias: textbooks, record/statistic books, biographics, how-to-do-it books, periodicals, films and filmstrips, letters, phone calls, personal interviews, surveys, polls, catalogs, and/or others?

For example, a fourth grade student interested in the weapons and vehicles used in Word War II read several adult-level books on this subject, including biographies, autobiographies, periodicals, and record books. He also conducted oral history interviews with local veterans of World War II, previewed films and filmstrips about the period, and collected letters from elderly citizens sent to them from their sons stationed overseas.

5	4	3	2	1	NA
To a great extent		Somewhat		To a limited extent	

Item 9 has seven different components which deal with an overall assessment of the product. No examples of students' work are provided for item 9. When completing the ratings for the overall assessment of a student's product, raters should attempt to evaluate the product in terms of their own values and certain characteristics that indicate the quality such as aesthetics, utility, and function of the overall contribution. In other words, raters are encouraged to consider the product as a whole (globally) in item 9 and to use their own judgment and rely upon their own guided subjective opinions when rating this item.

Because of the difficulty of developing a single instrument that will be universally applicable to all types of products, instances occur when some of the items do not apply to specific products. For that reason, a category entitled "Not Applicable" was added to the 1–5 Likert-type scale of items 1–8. For example, in a creative writing product (play, poem, novel) either the Level of Resources (item 3) or the Diversity of Resources (item 4) might not apply if the student is writing directly from his/her own experiences. This Not Applicable category is used very rarely in most rating situations and was not included in the overall assessment of the product (item 9), which uses a 1–4 Likert-type scale.

To examine content validity further, the form was evaluated by several recognized national authorities in the field of education of the gifted and in educational research. It was also distributed to 20 experienced teachers of the gifted in Connecticut. The authorities were asked carefully to assess the content of the form for omissions, clarity, and duplications. They were also asked for suggestions which would improve the form. Very few suggestions or omissions were mentioned by the experts, and the form was modified only slightly.

Reliability

Interrater Agreement. Interrater agreement was determined in two separate phases. In the first phase, 19 raters familiar with the field of education of the gifted (many of the raters were resource room teachers of the gifted) rated an original book on skunks, the product of a first grader. No explanations of the scale or the instructions were given; raters were simply given a copy of the *SPAF* and the product. They were also asked to assess the *SPAF* for language clarity, duplication, ease of instructions, and omissions (a further check on content validity). In other words, rater training was accomplished through the three pages of instructions which accompany the form. This was considered to be important for future use of the instrument, which is intended to be independent of formal in-service training.

After the phase one field test, the *Student Product Assessment Form* was revised according to interrater agreement percentages. Items 2, 6, and 7, which did not receive an agreement percentage of 80%, were revised and refined; one key concept in item 9 was eliminated and replaced with an item that three raters had listed as an omission. In the phase two field test, 22 raters (19 of the phase one group and 3 additional teachers of the gifted) rated a second product (an original local historical walking tour of a Connecticut city) and a third product (a novel written by a sixth grade student). On the second product, interrater agreement of 100% was achieved for 12 of the 15 items. The other 3 items achieved agreement percentages of 86.4, 90.9, and 95.5. The nature of the third product (the novel) made it more difficult to attain interrater agreement above 80% in two areas, level of resources and diversity of resources. However, all other agreement percentages were above 80%, and 90% agreement was achieved for 10 of the 15 items.

Stability

An additional consideration addressed was the extent to which the ratings would be stable over time. Stability reliability was determined by having the same raters assess product two (the historic walking tour) approximately 2 weeks after the first assessment. Almost identical responses and percentages were recorded. A correlation of + .96 was achieved between the first and second assessment of product two.

Interrater Reliability

A final phase of the reliability check was the generation of interrater reliabilities for 20 different products listed in Table 1. The products represented five different product types including Scientific ($n = 7$), Creative Writing ($n = 5$), Social Studies ($n = 5$), Audio-Visual ($n = 2$) and Interdisciplinary ($n = 1$). The products were submitted for assessment to staff members in three public school programs for gifted students in Connecticut. Four experienced teachers of the gifted were asked to evaluate the products using the *Student Product Assessment Form*. The products varied in format, subject matter, age of the student who completed them, and final form. Some products were accompanied by a completed management plan (a contract-like form used in some programs for the gifted). Other products were accompanied by the completed student guide that is an optional segment of the *Student Product Assessment Form*.

In some instances, the raters interviewed the student who had completed the product before evaluating it. Other times, the raters evaluated the final product simply by examining it without interviewing the student. This was considered essential for the generalizability of the instrument since it will be used in all of these situations.

To obtain the interrater reliabilities, the technique described by Ebel (1951) was utilized which intercorrelates the ratings obtained from different raters (see Guilford, 1954, pp. 395–397). The ratings of the four separate raters were correlated for each item presented in the *SPAF* as well as on the subtotals of Items 1 through 8, Items 9 A-G, and on the total rating of the items. Since each of the raters rated 20 products on 15 different traits, intercorrelations of the ratings of the products from all possible pairs of ratings were obtained. Table 2 presents the interrater reliability results of the mean reliability for one rater as well as four raters, on the nine different items. Also included are the subtotals and total rating of the *Student Product Assessment Form*.

It should be noted that two key concepts, Audience and Original Contribution, had lower reliability when evaluated by one rather than when evaluated by four raters. Since *SPAF* will often be used by single raters in the future, those two areas will need further examination.

Table 1   Listing of Products by Type Used to Generate Interrater Reliability

Type[a]		
4	1.	A weekly television show, "All Kinds of Kids," which is directed, produced, and filmed by a group of gifted students.
1	2.	A filmstrip on topology.
2	3.	A short story.
1	4.	A nonfictional book on pond life in Connecticut.
1	5.	A book on skunks.
3	6.	A genealogical investigation of a family and resulting book.
1	7.	A scientific investigation of mapping pond life resulting in a photo essay and book.
3	8.	An historical investigation and recreation of the "Battle of the Bulge."
1	9.	A model solar home.
1	10.	A reflector telescope.
5	11.	A filmstrip on computers and their history.
3	12.	A study on the attitudes of school and community toward the E.R.A.
3	13.	An historical walking tour of a city.
2	14.	A short novel.
2	15.	An autobiographical creative writing effort.
3	16.	An investigate study of a political issue in a community.
2	17.	A book of poetry.
2	18.	A novel entitled *Slave Boy*.
1	19.	A solar collector.
4	20.	A documentary film on sign language.

[a]Scale for Types of Products
   1 - Scientific   4 - Audio-visual
   2 - Creative Writing   5 - Interdisciplinary
   3 - Social Studies

The higher interrater reliability should be examined with the realization that the products submitted for evaluation were from three outstanding programs for gifted and talented students. The teachers who submitted products often chose them for their high quality. It could be that less superior products will be associated with lower reliabilities. Future data will be collected in this area. In summary, this section has described the development of the *Student Product Assessment Form*. Content validity procedures were presented and reliability assessment procedures (interrater agreement, stability, and interrater reliability) were described.

USES OF THE STUDENT PRODUCT ASSESSMENT FORM

An almost universal characteristic of students of all ages is a desire to know how they will be evaluated or "graded." We would like to begin by saying that we strongly discourage the formal grading of students' creative products. No

Table 2   Student Product Assessment Form

*Interrater Reliability of One Rater and Four
Raters on Individual Items and Totals[a]*

Items	1 Rater	4 Raters
1. Early Statement of Purpose	1.000	1.000
2. Problem Focusing	1.000	1.000
3. Level of Resources	.973	.993
4. Diversity of Resources	.963	.990
5. Appropriateness of Resources	.983	.996
6. Logic, Sequence, and Transition	.779	.934
7. Action Orientation	.913	.997
8. Audience	.533	.820
Subtotal Key Concepts 1 – 8	.994	.998
9. Overall Assessment		
A. Originality of the Idea	.778	.993
B. Achieved Objectives Stated in Plan	.789	.937
C. Advanced Familiarity with Subject	1.000	1.000
D. Quality Beyond Age/Grade Level	.912	.971
E. Care, Attention to Detail, etc.	1.000	1.000
F. Time, Effort, Energy	.875	.966
G. Original Contribution	.390	.718
Subtotal Key Concepts 9A – G	.924	.980
Total of All Items on *SPAF*	.961	.990

[a]Note that these data are based upon 20 products rated by four people.

letter grade, number, or percent can accurately reflect the comprehensive types of knowledge, creativity, and task commitment that are developed within the context of a creative product. At the same time, however, evaluation and feedback are an important part of the overall process of promoting growth through this type of enrichment experience, and students should be thoroughly oriented in the procedures that will be used to evaluate their work.

The best way to help students understand the ways in which their work will be evaluated is to conduct a series of orientation sessions organized around *SPAF*. Two or three examples of completed student products that highlight varying levels of quality on the respective scales from the *SPAF* instrument will help students to gain an appreciation for both the factors involved in the assessment and the examples of the manifestation of each factor.

The evaluation of student products in many gifted programs has been carried out in a random and rather haphazard manner. Often, no evaluation occurs and a valuable opportunity to provide feedback and to discuss future ideas for subsequent work is lost. If *SPAF* is used to evaluate completed student products, the cover sheet (see Figure 1) could be filed in students' permanent record folders, providing an academic portfolio of their creative products from the primary grades through high school. Since so many gifted programming models include the development of student products (Betts, 1986; Clifford, Runions, & Smyth, 1986; Feldhusen & Kolloff, 1986; Feldhusen & Robinson, 1986; Kaplan, 1986; Renzulli & Reis, 1985), the evaluation of such products would seem not only logical, but advisable.

REFERENCES

Amabile, T. M. (1983). *The social psychology of creativity.* New York: Springer-Verlag.

Archambault, F. X., & Gubbins, E. J. (1980). [Student product rating scale]. Unpublished.

Bessemer, S. P., & O'Quin, K. (1987). Creative product analysis: Testing a model by developing a judging instrument. In S. G. Isaksen (Ed.), *Frontiers of creativity research: Beyond the basics* (pp. 341–357). Buffalo, NY: Bearly Limited.

Bessemer, S. P., & Treffinger, D. J. (1981). Analysis of creative products: Review and synthesis. *Journal of Creative Behaviors, 15,* 159–179.

Betts, G. T. (1986). The autonomous learner model. In J. S. Renzulli (Ed.), *Systems and models for developing programs for the gifted and talented* (pp. 27–56). Mansfield Center, CT: Creative Learning Press.

Callahan, C. M. (1980). [Student product rating scale]. Unpublished.

Clifford, J. A., Runions, T., & Smyth, E. (1986). The learning enrichment service (LES): A participatory model for gifted adolescents. In J. S. Renzulli (Ed.), *Systems and models for developing programs for the gifted and talented* (pp. 92–125). Mansfield Center, CT: Creative Learning Press.

Council for Exceptional Children. (1979). Sample instruments for the evaluation of programs for the gifted and talented. Bureau of Educational Research, U-7, Storrs Hall, University of Connecticut, Storrs, CT 06269.

Ebel, R. L. (1951). Estimation of the reliability of ratings. *Psychometric, 16,* 407–424.

Feldhusen, J. F., & Kolloff, M. B. (1986). The Purdue three-stage enrichment model for gifted education at the elementary level. In J. S. Renzulli (Ed.), *Systems and models for developing programs for the gifted and talented* (pp. 126–152). Mansfield Center, CT: Creative Learning Press.

Feldhusen, J. F., & Robinson, A. (1986). The Purdue Secondary Model for gifted and talented youth. In J. S. Renzulli (Ed.), *Systems and models for developing programs for the gifted and talented* (pp. 126–152). Mansfield Center, CT: Creative Learning Press.

Getzels, J., & Csikszentmihalyi, M. (1976). *The creative vision: A longitudinal study of problem-finding in art.* New York: Wiley-Interscience.

Guilford, J. P. (1954). *Psychometric methods.* New York: McGraw Hill.

Jackson, P., & Messick, S. (1965). The person, the product and the response: Conceptual problems in the assessment of creativity. *Journal of Personality, 33,* 309–329.

Kaplan, S. N. (1986). The grid: A model to construct differentiated curriculum for the gifted. In J. S. Renzulli (Ed.), *Systems and models for developing programs for the gifted and talented* (pp. 180–193). Mansfield Center, CT: Creative Learning Press.

MacKinnon, D. W. (1987). Some critical issues for future research in creativity. In S. G. Isaksen (Ed.), *Frontiers of creativity research* (pp. 120–130). Buffalo, NY: Bearly Limited.

Reis, S. M. (1981). *An analysis of the productivity of gifted students participating in programs using the revolving door identification model.* Unpublished doctoral dissertation, University of Connecticut, Storrs.

Renzulli, J. S. (1977). *The enrichment triad model: A guide for developing defensible programs for the gifted* (pp. 429–460). Mansfield Center, CT: Creative Learning Press.

Renzulli, J. S., & Reis, S. M. (1985). *The schoolwide enrichment model: A comprehensive plan for educational excellence.* Mansfield Center, CT: Creative Learning Press.

Rhodes, M. (1987). An analysis of creativity. In S. G. Isaksen (Ed.), *Frontiers of creativity research* (pp. 216–222). Buffalo, NY: Bearly Limited.

Sobel, R. S., & Rothenberg, A. (1980). Artistic creation as stimulated by superimposed versus separated visual images. *Journal of Personality and Social Psychology, 39,* 953–961.

Treffinger, D. J. (1986). Fostering effective, independent learning through individualized programming. In J. S. Renzulli (Ed.), *Systems and models for developing programs for the gifted and talented.* (pp. 429–460). Mansfield Center, CT: Creative Learning Press.

Treffinger, D. J. (1987). Research on creativity assessment. In S. G. Isaksen (Ed.), *Frontiers of creativity research* (pp. 103–119). Buffalo, NY: Bearly Limited.

Tuttle, F. B. (1980). *Evaluation report for Concord MA.* Project Gather and Project Lift. Concord School System, Concord, MA.

Westberg, K. L. (1990). *The effects of instruction in the inventing process on students' development of inventions.* Unpublished doctoral dissertation, University of Connecticut, Storrs, CT.

6

Making Evaluation Work: One School District's Experience

Linda D. Avery & Joyce Van Tassel-Baska

The College of William and Mary

Barbara O'Neill

Greenwich Public Schools

Given the paucity of evaluation studies of gifted programs in the literature, this article shares the experiences of the Greenwich Public Schools in sponsoring an external evaluation of their K - 8 program for gifted and talented youngsters. The article explains the methodology used in the evaluation, discusses findings and recommendations, and describes how the results were translated into program improvement efforts. Also addressed are the evaluators' observations about lessons learned in the process of the evaluation; these lessons reflect on the utility of information gathered.

Editor's Note: From Avery, L. D., VanTassel-Baska, J., & O'Neill, B. (1997). Making evaluation work: One school district's experience. *Gifted Child Quarterly, 41*(4), 124-132. © 1997 National Association for Gifted Children. Reprinted with permission.

W hile the field of gifted education has advocated evaluation as a central part of program development for a number of years, there is a paucity of studies in literature to provide insight on what works and what does not work in gifted programs (VanTassel-Baska, 1998). Without a fundamental database on a program as it evolves, meaningful program improvement is not a possibility. Moreover, the field can be led to employ any and all new ideas unproductively if student impact is not systematically assessed. Thus, it is a rare event when a school district displays conscious and sophisticated understanding of the link between program improvement and evaluation as strongly as is seen in the case of Greenwich, Connecticut. The insights afforded through their experience offer much to advance our understanding of the linkage between evaluation and program improvement.

Greenwich can be characterized as an affluent suburban school system with high student test scores and a slowly changing demographic base. The district has provided enriched educational experiences to gifted students for over thirty years, targeting the subject areas of language arts and mathematics through different organizational models at the elementary level in Grades 3 through 5. Advanced courses in mathematics, English, and humanities with additional interdisciplinary seminars are offered at the middle school level in Grades 6 through 8. High school programs, although not included in this study, incorporate a rich array of honors. Advanced Placement courses and opportunities for independent study.

Although the district does not have a full-time coordinator for gifted education, the district does periodically contract with outside consultants to review program effectiveness and to help frame program development issues to improve the quality of services. If the school is viewed as a learning community, Greenwich is willing to struggle with asking the right questions. To their credit, this struggle involves the sometimes painful, but always meaningful, contribution of an ardent parent constituency.

The program evaluation reported in this paper focused on two major questions:

1. To what extent are gifted programs effectively differentiated from regular education programs?

2. What are the attitudes of critical stakeholders in modifying and/or strengthening different elements of the current program?

Although these questions do not address the traditional linch pin of student performance, they nevertheless afford an opportunity to address necessary and related variables, and they speak to genuine program development interests.

Putting the Research to Use

The sharing of the results of this study is intended to help illuminate effective gifted program evaluation procedures. This particular design focused on classroom observations, parent, teacher; and student perceptions of impact, and parent and educator perspectives on different program elements. Although student performance data were not available during the evaluation, the process convinced stakeholder groups of the importance of adding this dimension to the database through the changes that were recommended. The evaluation confirms many of the recommendations made by other researchers about how to make evaluation findings useful and provides some additional suggestions. Of particular interest is the need to use multiple channels to share the results, rather than over-relying on the written report as the vehicle to inspire recommended modifications.

A review of the recent literature indicates that effective evaluations of gifted programs continue to be sporadic and lack evaluation designs and procedures which are robust, meaningful, thorough, and well funded (Tomlinson & Callahan, 1993). The rarity and haphazard nature of gifted program evaluations is further confirmed by Silky and Reading (1992). Although gifted programs should not be evaluated solely to determine whether or not they are needed (Callahan, 1995), evaluation should play a critical role in assessing the worthiness of program differentiation and the level of program impact on gifted students. According to Southern (1992) in a time of shrinking resources and reallocation of priorities, educators must demonstrate to their constituents that programs and services for gifted learners are important and valuable.

Across the field as a whole, progress in collecting valuable data proceeds much like the creation of a mosaic with each tile adding another component to the big picture. Miller (1991) attributes the idiosyncratic nature of these contributions in part to the variable definitions of three key terms: giftedness, gifted programs, and evaluation. She suggests that the existing evaluation literature is questionable and "only hints at the effects" of programs and policies. In a synthesis of evaluation studies on programs for disadvantaged gifted students, House and Lapan (1994) noted that few actual studies draw on the scholarship from all three areas: evaluation, gifted education, and disadvantaged learners. They further acknowledged the value of the current trend to combine quantitative and qualitative data and recommended greater use of multiple indicators and more emphasis on formative evaluation.

Other contributions have been made in relation to gifted program evaluation and research. VanTassel-Baska, Willis, and Meyer (1989) conducted a controlled study of a self-contained gifted program in South Bend using a pre-post design with multiple outcome measures which confirmed student gains in cognitive ability and higher levels of satisfaction with school life for students served by the program. A nonexperimental retrospective study of the long-term effects of pull-out enrichment programs using the Purdue Three-Stage Model revealed the positive perceptions of program recipients in terms of improved thinking skills and problem-solving abilities (Moon, Feldhusen, & Dillon, 1994). Carter's study (1992) on the effects of a northern Colorado gifted program on independent learning showed disappointing results in that statistically significant differences were not detected between the participants and comparison groups.

Although classroom observation is not widely reported in the gifted education literature on program evaluation, a national study of educational practices used with gifted students in regular classrooms included both classroom observation and teacher surveys (Westberg, Archambault, Jr., Dobyns, & Salvin, 1993). The study reported no instructional and curricular differentiation in the vast majority of classroom activities.

To describe current gifted program evaluation practices, Hunsaker and Callahan (1993) reviewed and analyzed seventy evaluation reports. All three of the promising practices noted in their study were incorporated into the Greenwich evaluation, namely 1) collecting data for program improvement not solely for accountability, 2) focusing on a number of key areas rather than settling for generalized program impressions, and 3) increasing utility by formulating action plans in response to the recommendations. Unfortunately, Tomlinson, Bland, and Moon (1993) decried that "the literature of gifted education is nearly mute on evaluation utility" (p. 183). It is partially within this context of effective utilization that the evaluation of the Greenwich gifted program best informs our knowledge about the processes which support program improvement at the local level.

METHODOLOGY

The general approach used to conduct this evaluation followed Stake's naturalistic evaluation model (1975). Key steps in Stake's model include talking with relevant publics to determine the right questions to explore, then designing or selecting instrumentation and methodology that will collect data on these identified issues. The first stage of the evaluation was the creation of focus groups, followed by summarizing the results of their discussions and feeding the results back to the participants for further reflection and clarification. Such ongoing communication was important to keep the evaluation process on center stage.

The evaluation design for the Greenwich gifted program included 1) observations of gifted and regular classrooms, 2) interviews with building principals and other key administrators, teachers of the gifted, and parent groups, 3) educator and parent surveys focusing on priorities for re-definition and expansion of the program, and 4) student, teacher and parent questionnaires on perceptions of program impact on the students. Using multiple data sources helped ensure that the evaluation responded to different stakeholders' viewpoints.

CLASSROOM OBSERVATION COMPONENT

Instrumentation

The classroom observation component responded to the question of the level of differentiation and employed a quasi-experimental method, comparing the results of observations across gifted and regular classrooms. This was the most rigorous component of the evaluation in terms of research and evaluation design.

Trained graduate students and center staff developed a *Classroom Observation Form* for the study which incorporated seven categories of observable content and instructional strategies and two categories of elements of educational reform. Categories were further subdivided into items for a total of 40 items across all categories. Table 1, which will be discussed in the Results section, enumerates the categories and items. Items were selected through a review of the literature on effective teaching practices with particular attention to gifted learners. Additional measures to strengthen reliability included pilot-testing the instrument, revising the instrument based on the results from the pilot, using a number of different trained individuals to conduct the observations, and drawing large sample sizes.

One hundred and fourteen classrooms were observed; 75 at the elementary level and 39 at the middle school level. At the elementary level, 39% of the classrooms were for gifted students and at the middle school level 31% were. Percentages were calculated for each item, and statistical tests of significance were performed using a Chi square; the results of forty 2X2 chi squares have been archived and are available from the authors.

Results

Of the nine major categories focusing on teaching behaviors and curriculum reform, there were no statistically significant differences between the gifted and regular classrooms. However, most trends in directionality were consistent with areas where differentiation would be expected, such as in the use of critical and creative thinking strategies. More surprising were the trends related to educational reform which also favored the gifted classrooms but showed very little penetration of the system in either type of programming.

Through the finer lens of the item level, statistically significant differences emerged. Nineteen of the 40 items favored the gifted classroom with 2 showing statistical significance. One of these items dealt with accelerated content and the other focused on the component of school reform dealing with problem-centered curricula. The results favored the regular classroom on 13 of the items with two additional items reflecting statistical significance: multicultural sensitivity and the use of lecture/discourse. No trends one way or the other were identified on 8 of the items. Table 1 provides a summary chart of the results of the administration of the Classroom Observation Form.

Implications

Although the differences between the gifted and the regular classrooms were not as deeply penetrating as one might anticipate, the high quality of the instructional staff in this district and the strong academic standing of the overall student population may explain the blurring of effects. It is also possible the instrument may not have been sensitive enough to detect real differences. This study found that traditional classrooms are more likely to incorporate the lecture mode while gifted classrooms offer accelerated content and greater evidence of critical and higher order thinking skills. Many of the other features that have historically defined gifted education experiences appear to have been absorbed into the general curriculum.

Even so, gifted classrooms are in the vanguard of incorporating elements of the educational reform movement. Curricula for high ability learners are fertile ground for embedding problem-based learning, organizing around key concepts, emphasizing depth, and facilitating interdisciplinarity. Surprisingly, in the Greenwich program, the gifted classrooms also demonstrated greater use of cooperative learning strategies and the hands-on use of manipulatives. While such learning enhancements are clearly intended for broader consumption, it may be through the adaptations made by teachers of the gifted that change in the educational experience as a whole is more vividly illuminated.

The recommendations from this component of the evaluation were to strive for greater levels of curriculum differentiation in gifted classrooms, to increase classroom extension experiences for gifted students, and to accentuate key elements of educational reform. Of particular concern was the need to strengthen evidence of multicultural sensitivity across the educational landscape.

PERCEPTIONS OF STUDENT IMPACT COMPONENT

Instrumentation

The student impact component of the Greenwich evaluation assessed perceptions of the program's effectiveness from the perspectives of three constituent groups: teachers of the gifted program (TAG), parents of students in the program, and the students themselves.

The *Student Impact Questionnaire* consisted of two rating scales which included both cognitive and affective indicators. Cognitive indicators included assessment of achievement in various subject matter areas, problem-solving ability, and communication skills. Affective indicators included self-esteem, tolerance, and feelings about the program. For each item on the instrument, means and modes based on the point scales were calculated for student, parent, and TAG teacher groups. Sufficient responses were secured from all groups to ascertain general patterns across the program, but responses were not evenly distributed across grade levels and buildings to warrant further disaggregation of the results.

Results

The findings of the student impact component were useful in determining areas of convergence and divergence in the perceptions of the program. Although teachers were consistently more favorable than students or parents, there was marked uniformity between teachers and students in their top ranked items. Both teachers and students perceived the program affected students' ability to think about complex ideas, to listen to others, to problem solve, and to be more creative.

In contrast, the parents' most favored response, dealing with impact on self-esteem, was not among the five most favored responses of teachers or students. Parents also, unlike teachers and students, showed neutrality on the item dealing with tolerance of others with different traits. Although differences in perception across the three groups of respondents were not dramatic, the discrepancies gave participants an opportunity to discuss the implications of the findings for the program when they were reconvened in focus groups.

Implications

The recommendation from this component of the evaluation was to strengthen the program design so that all constituents understood the expectations for the program and recognized that both cognitive and affective student gains should be of universal interest. In order to measure student gains, the curriculum needed greater standardization across school buildings, and assessment instruments needed to be identified and approved. A significant outgrowth of this component was the commitment made by district administration to collect empirical evidence of student performance tied to subsequent curriculum changes made in the program. The collection of stakeholders' perceptions thus led to the recognition that learning gains should be incorporated into an ongoing evaluation design for the program.

EDUCATOR AND PARENT SURVEY COMPONENT

Instrumentation

The use of the *Educator and Parent Questionnaires* corresponded directly to the second question that framed the evaluation, namely what changes, if any, were needed in restructuring or refining the current program. Although two

Table 1 Summary Chart of the Classroom Observation Form

No.	Category/Item	Favors Gifted	Favors Regular	Same
1.	Curriculum Planning			
	A. Written Lesson Plan		X	
	B. Communicated Purpose of Learning		X	
	C. Adherence to Plan		X	
	D. Digression from Plan	X		
2.	Individual Differences			
	A. Appropriate Challenges	X		
	B. Differences in Learning Ability		X	
	C. Multicultural Sensitivity*		X	
	D. Different Learning Modes	X		
3.	Versatility in Strategies			
	A. Lecture/Discourse*		X	
	B. Discussion	X		
	C. Student Application	X		
	D. Use of Technology			X
	E. Large Group Interaction			X
	F. Small Group Interaction	X		
	G. Individualized Activities	X		
4.	Critical/Advanced Thinking			
	A. Evaluates Situations/Problems	X		
	B. Compares and Contrasts Ideas	X		
	C. Generalizes Concrete to Abstract			X
	D. Debate/Develop Argument			X
	E. Cross Disciplinary Comparisons		X	
	F. Acquires Accelerated Content**	X		

No.	Category/Item	Favors Gifted	Favors Regular	Same
5.	Creative Thinking/Problem Solv.			
	A. Brainstorm Ideas			X
	B. Explore or Advan. New Conclus.		X	
	C. Alternate Modes of Expression		X	
	D. Self Select Topics for More Explor.		X	
6.	Learning Environments			
	A. Motivational Techniques		X	
	B. Energy and Enthusiasm		X	
	C. Pace Instruc. Based on Readiness			X
7.	Classroom Extensions			
	A. Assigns Homework	X		
	B. Alternative Ideas to Pursue			X
	C. Special Projects Easily Implem.		X	
	D. Refer. to People/Materials Suppl.			X
8.	Curriculum Reform Elements			
	A. Problem-Centered*	X		
	B. Flexibility	X		
	C. Emphasizes Depth	X		
	D. Interdisciplinary in Design	X		
	E. Organizes Access to Key Concepts	X		
9.	Instructional Reform Strategy			
	A. Hands-on Use of Manipulatives	X		
	B. Cooperative Learning	X		
	C. Inquiry-oriented/Const. of Mean.	X		

*p < .05   **p < .01

separate 33-item questionnaires were crafted for use with these educators and parents, the majority of items were duplicated on each instrument with the specific phrasing tailored to the targeted population. This pairing of items again allowed for identification of convergence and divergence of opinion between educational personnel and the parent public.

The items on these questionnaires covered a wide range of issues including identification parameters, organizational/grouping arrangements, curriculum content and instructional strategies, staff development opportunities, parent involvement, student and program evaluation, and overall program satisfaction. Examples of items are presented in Appendix A. Most of the items were multiple choice although some allowed the selection of an *Other* category filled in at the respondent's discretion. The analysis used percentages displayed with bar graphs to compare the responses across the two groups. No statistical procedures were used to ascertain significance.

Results

In spite of the length of the instrument, over 550 questionnaires were returned from the 13 school buildings included in the study. The return rate on the *Parent Questionnaire* was 58%; for the *Educator Questionnaire*, the return rate was 43%.

The gifted program coordinator followed up with the educator group to stimulate the return rate, but the size of the instrument (about 6 pages of fine print) may have discouraged responses.

The analysis compared parent and educator responses for all items and displayed the distribution for selected items on graphs. The evaluation report provided a narrative discussion of the results by item and fed these analyses into the recommendations. The major findings by program component or function and related conclusions are described in Appendix B.

Implications

The recommendations described in the final report incorporated data from all components of the evaluation effort but did not tie directly to the conclusions in all cases. For example, recommendations about staffing were the outgrowth of the conclusions rather than directly stated in them. The eight recommendations suggested the district should:

1. Establish a full-time position for gifted program coordination.

2. Revise and standardize the criteria for participation in building level gifted programs across the district.

3. Phase in expansion of identification of the K - 2 gifted students over the next five years.

4. Develop a plan for the provision of gifted program core services to all participating schools. Core services should be the minimum offerings uniform across all buildings in the district.

5. Provide a full-time gifted program staff person in each building.

6. Develop district guidelines for supplementary services to be offered at the building level based on priorities established through an agreed upon process; consider piloting a science program for gifted students in interested buildings.

7. Develop materials and communication strategies that convey effectively the nature and extent of the gifted program.

8. Develop assessment strategies for gifted student performance that emphasize both cognitive and affective domains.

All but one of these recommendations were incorporated into the plan of action that emerged from the evaluation effort. Although the district determined that a full-time coordinator was not financially feasible at that time, the district did increase the number of TAG teachers at the elementary level.

Summary Reporting Mechanisms

Dissemination of the evaluation findings used several mechanisms. Draft reports were shared with program administration to correct errors and to eliminate educational jargon. A formal school board presentation was made by the researcher; and a town meeting was held for the community. Special sessions to discuss the results of the evaluation and the suggested three-year plan of action were held with principals, task force members, TAG teachers, and others interested in the outcome of the study. The web of formal and informal meetings with key constituents was more valuable than the written report in promoting utilization of findings. Although a final written report was prepared in compliance with the terms of the contract, the effort made to provide feedback at multiple junctures during the evaluation and the encapsulation of findings onto overheads and hand-outs to present to constituents helped ensure that participants understood the results. The commitment to sharing and marketing the results of the evaluation, as well as the endemic interest of the district itself in the evaluation effort, contributed to the approval of major program enhancements. The juxtaposition of the evaluation report with a program development plan enabled the district to discuss openly the limitations of the program as well as showcase their investment in making recommended changes.

Implications for Conducting Evaluations Actively Utilized

The evaluation effort for this program leads us to some observations about enhancing the likelihood that evaluation findings will be meaningful and useful to program decision makers. Our experience suggests the following:

1. The evaluation must be linked at a practical, not an ideal level, to program development needs. The evaluator must recognize where the program is in its current evolution and determine a reasonable framework for the next level

of development. In other words, the evaluation should frame reasonable next steps to take. If the evaluation focuses on the gap between where the program is and what the "ideal" program should look like, the district may see too much distance to cover. Conversely, if the recommendations are too close to the current manifestation of the program, they may be ignored and seen as unnecessary. Because a delicate balance is warranted, great care must be exercised in understanding and synthesizing the history of the program, its current parameters, and the perceptions of stakeholders regarding the purpose of the evaluation.

2. The evaluation must be interactive to diffuse potential polarization of constituencies. Unlike quantitative research paradigms which require a high level of objectivity in measuring results, an evaluation may be most useful if it is modulated by the interests of the prime audiences. An effective evaluation should create adequate opportunities for voicing divergent, even hostile, opinions and incorporate forums for processing resistance or resentment. Even in districts with a high level of investment in and commitment to gifted education, there are elements of controversy inflamed in the evaluation process. In serving as a lightning rod for such controversy, the evaluator must step into the dialogue and become a participant in the process at vulnerable junctures. If the district has to stand alone to absorb this antagonism, the consequences of making changes will be weighed against maintaining the status quo.

3. The evaluation must be flexible and fluid in the recommendations that are generated. It is important to frame recommendations that allow the district administration some room for maneuvering in response to the evaluation. Offering a variety of recommendations, or a menu of some options for their consideration, helps a district to move forward but also juggle the realities of political and financial constraints. In addition to the language used to couch the recommendation or to explain the need for the recommendation, the follow up meetings should be open to allow discussion of alternative pathways to the ultimate goal of high quality educational services to gifted and talented youth.

Implications for Local Programs

Many of the questions with which the Greenwich gifted program found itself grappling are not unlike the questions faced by other school systems across the country. Thus, the articulation of them may lead to greater awareness of important steps toward program improvement. These critical issues are:

1. In the real world of schools, the distinction between gifted students and the general cohort is blurry. Because "giftedness" in the context of educational offerings is a relative, not an absolute phenomenon, professionals in gifted education are cautious about identification strategies and cut-off scores that exclude children who in other settings might be included. Casting a wide identification net leads to expanding the range of giftedness so that more children are selected for program inclusion. The wider the range of abilities of children in the program, the more diffuse the program becomes until it begins to look

like the regular curriculum, particularly in districts with student bodies scoring in the upper percentile ranges. Our well-intentioned decisions about identification and placement lead to complications in ensuring differentiation of services.

2. Gifted education must be tied fundamentally to an accelerated and enriched core curriculum across school buildings at the district level. The enactment of such a core curriculum serves as an anchor for the elements of the educational experience which meet the cognitive and affective needs of the gifted learner. Without committing to certain differentiated curricular components warranted by the needs of talented youth, we are vulnerable to offering inconsistent, ad hoc, discretionary interventions seen both by advocates and opponents of gifted education as frills.

3. The curriculum offered through gifted education must be articulated vertically across grade levels and laterally to the general curriculum. The scope and sequence expectations for the gifted curricular offerings and the linkages and/or interface that occurs with the regular education program should be made explicit. There is a real need to discuss how curriculum experiences for the gifted connect to each other and to the regular school curriculum through specific subject matter, the language of local schools and the new national standards work. Curriculum articulation is the process which drives this discussion at the district level.

4. Without standardized identification procedures across schools or prescribed curricular interventions linked to the total educational framework, gifted services are easily co-opted by other systemic needs. Teachers of the gifted are pulled into other programmatic initiatives; special seminars are expanded to the whole student body; financial supports are redirected to more generalized service gaps. When the philosophical infrastructure is weak, it is easy to plunder the bounty.

5. In the current climate of site-based management, the struggle between centralization versus building autonomy is exacerbated. In the absence or ambiguity of central administration policies or guidelines, building administrators are free to craft programs which vary in their range and quality. This reinforces competition among school principals, stirs up parent unrest, and undermines the integrity of the district's commitment to gifted education. It is critical that a consensus-building model be used to reframe the program evolution challenges.

Identifying such issues in the abstract is far easier than translating them into reality. Our experiences in Greenwich suggest that these perspectives can be promulgated in open forums and that the programmatic decisions reached in the context of such debate can strengthen and nourish the vision of gifted education. In sharing our experiences and observations with the field, we hope to contribute to the literature base on utilization of evaluations as well as assist other professionals in identifying pitfalls which short-change the impact of evaluation efforts.

SUMMARY

The opportunity to collaborate on the evaluation of the Greenwich gifted program led to many insights at both conceptual and operational levels. Because there is little consensus in the field of gifted education about who should be served and through what organizational models, it is not surprising that implementation at the local school district level is fragmented and inconsistent. Even in a district with the sophistication of Greenwich, where the staff are consumately competent and the parents are involved and knowledgeable, the critical issues are easily clouded. Only through constant vigilance, examination, and disclosure of key program practices can local programs identify and confront shortcomings. It is through such scrutiny and the subsequent program changes that the integrity of gifted education is retained and strengthened.

REFERENCES

Callahan, C. M. (1995). Using evaluation to improve programs for the gifted. *The School Administrator, 52*(4), 22–24.

Carter, K. (1992). A model for evaluating programs for the gifted under non-experimental conditions, *Journal for the Education of the Gifted, 15,* 266–283.

House, E. R., & Lapan, S. (1994). Evaluation of programs for disadvantaged gifted students. *Journal for the Education of the Gifted, 17,* 441–466.

Hunsaker, S. L., & Callahan, C. M. (1993). Evaluation of gifted programs: Current practices. *Journal for the Education of the Gifted, 16,* 190–200.

Miller, A. B. (1991). Evaluating gifted programs; the state of the art. *Gifted Education International, 7,* 133–139.

Moon, S. M., Feldhusen, J. E., & Dillon, D. R. (1994). Long-term effects of an enrichment program based on the Purdue three-stage model. *Gifted Child Quarterly, 38,* 38–48.

Silky, W., & Reading, J. (1992). REDSIL: A fourth generation evaluation model for gifted education programs. *Roeper Review, 15,* 67–69.

Southern, W. T. (1992). Lead us not into temptation: Issues in evaluating the effectiveness of gifted programs. In *Challenges in gifted education: Developing potential and investing in knowledge for the 21st century* (pp. 103–108). Columbus, OH: Ohio Department of Education.

Stake, R. (1975). *Program evaluation.* Occasional Paper Series. Kalamazoo, MI: Evaluation Center, Western Michigan University.

Tomlinson, C., & Callahan, C. M. (1993). Planning effective evaluations for programs for the gifted. *Roeper Review 17,* 46–51.

Tomlinson, C., Bland, L., & Moon, T. (1993). Evaluation utilization: A review of the literature with implications for gifted education. *Journal for the Education of the Gifted, 16,* 171–189.

VanTassel-Baska, J. (Ed.). (1998). *Excellence in educating gifted and talented learners* (3rd ed.). Denver, CO: Love.

VanTassel-Baska, J., Willis, G. B., & Meyer, D. (1989). Evaluation of a full-time self-contained class for gifted students. *Gifted Child Quarterly, 33,* 7–10.

Westberg, K. L., Archambault, Jr., F. X., Dobyns, S. M., Salvin, T. J. (1993). *An observational study of instructional and curricular practices used with gifted and talented students in regular classrooms.* Storrs, CT: NRCGT.

Appendix A

Sample Items from Educator Questionnaires

Number   Item

4. Are you familiar with the identification process used to select students for participation in gifted program services?

      ☐ YES   ☐ NO

5. If you answered YES above, which statement best describes your perception of the process.

- ☐ The process is fair and targets a reasonable number of students for participation in the program.
- ☐ The process is too broad and dilutes the effectiveness of the program.
- ☐ The process is too narrow and excludes students who should benefit.
- ☐ The process is too inconsistent and does not provide for uniform procedures from grade level to grade level or school to school.
- ☐ Other (please specify): _____

9. If your school district decided to offer a uniform approach to TAG programming in language arts and math and your particular school building already had the selected approach in place, what would be your FIRST preference for the next area of expansion of programming?

- ☐ I would like to see programming added in the area of science.
- ☐ I would like to see programming added in the area of creative development.
- ☐ I would like to see talent development and support in the area of physical education or kinestheology.
- ☐ I would like to see interdisciplinary enrichment activities that focus on critical thinking skills.
- ☐ My school does not have language arts and math in place yet so this would be my first priority.
- ☐ Other (please specify): _____

11. Which statement best reflects your opinion regarding whether the curriculum in your school is sufficiently challenging for gifted students?

- ☐ The regular program curriculum is challenging.
- ☐ The TAG curriculum is challenging.
- ☐ Both the regular and the TAG curricula are challenging.
- ☐ Neither the regular nor the TAG curricula are challenging.

Appendix B

Major Findings	Conclusions

1. Identification Process

A. Seventy-four percent of parents and sixty-five percent of educators claimed familiarity with the identification process.

B. Over forty percent of parents and fifty percent of teachers expressed dissatisfaction with the identification process.

C. Blocks of parents and educators showed concerns about the identification of low income and students with disabilities.

The district needs to revise the identification process to accommodate different sub-populations and to create an allowance for building flexibility

2. Curriculum and Instruction

A. Forty-one percent of educators and twenty percent of parents were unable to report awareness of curriculum differentiation.

B. Both parents and educators recognized the emphasis on critical and complex thinking embedded in the program.

C. Almost seventy percent of educators, but only forty percent of parents rated the local curriculum as sufficiently challenging.

D. The need for greater content acceleration was identified by twelve percent of parents but only three percent of educators.

E. These results complemented the information retrieved through the classroom observation component of the study.

The district needs to enhance the distinctions between regular and gifted education at the classroom level, strengthen classroom extension experiences, and increase attention to individual learning differences.

3. Organization

A. Both parents and educators expressed support for variety of organizational arrangements to support gifted education with seventy percent of parents favoring special classes or pull-out programs in language arts and mathematics.

B. Modest support existed for extended programming to K-2.

C. Sixty-four percent of both groups supported offering a uniform set of basic gifted services across schools coupled with additional options for school specialization.

D. Seventy-seven percent of parents and sixty percent of educators supported expansion in the range of gifted services offered.

E. Almost sixty percent of parents indicated that gifted education teachers should provide direct instruction to gifted students outside the regular classroom.

The district needs to move to a multi-level service delivery model that encompasses regular classroom enhancement, core academic offerings in language arts and mathematics, expanded program options such as science, creative arts, or early childhood selected at the building level.

4. Staff Development

A. Eighty-five percent of educators left that all teachers could benefit from staff development related to programming for gifted students.

B. Gifted education teachers and regular education teachers showed the same preferences in regards to joint training.

C. Eighty-eight percent of educators who attended previous training sessions rate their experiences as adequate or excellent.

The district needs to focus staff development on differentiation of the core services. Staff development should include opportunities for all teachers and provide a parent education component as well.

(Continued)

Appendix B (Continued)

Major Findings	Conclusions
D. Most parents expressed an interest in attending informational or training events related to motivating or supporting gifted students.	
5. Assessment and Evaluation	
A. Both parents and educators identified the use of narrative reports as a key strategy to provide feedback on student performance. Pre- and post-tests of content also rated favorably across both groups.	The district needs to consider student assessment approaches that measure student growth. Program changes that occur as a result of the study should be closely monitored.
B. Both parents and educators agreed that parents should have periodic involvement in evaluating their child's performance.	
C. Both groups recognized the importance of annual feedback as well as a longitudinal perspective.	
6. Communication	
A. Many parents and educators rated communication as adequate or better but sizable percentages awarded ratings in the poor range.	The district needs to improve communication efforts through the use of written materials and when appropriate, face-to-face meetings. Specific strategies should be reviewed by members of relevant groups prior to adoption.
B. Thirty percent of educators rated the communication between gifted and regular education teachers as poor.	
C. Both parents and teachers favored written methods of communication.	

7

An Evaluation of the Catalyst Program: Consultation and Collaboration in Gifted Education

Mary S. Landrum

University of Virginia

A recent evaluation of the Catalyst Program, a resource consultation and collaboration program in gifted education, was conducted in order to investigate the effects of student academic performance and teacher competencies, as well as the effectiveness of the consulting process applied to gifted education. In a two-year pilot program, general educators and gifted education specialists at 10 elementary schools in a large, urban

Editor's Note: From Landrum, M. S. (2001). An evaluation of the catalyst program: Consultation and collaboration in gifted education. *Gifted Child Quarterly, 45*(2), 139-151. © 2001 National Association for Gifted Children. Reprinted with permission.

school district consulted and collaborated with one another to provide differentiated educational experiences to gifted learners. Results indicate that the model was an effective service delivery strategy for providing differentiated education to gifted learners, had positive spill-over effects for the entire school, led to a redefined role of the gifted education specialist, and initiated an articulation of the nature of the consulting process when applied to gifted education.

There are inherent limitations to traditional gifted education service delivery strategies. For example, pull-out programs tend to operate separately from the regular education programs and serve students on a limited basis. In addition, segregation of gifted services can contribute to perceptions of elitism. Further, the pull-out program only serves the unique needs of gifted learners sometimes. In the pull-out approach, gifted learners often leave the classroom at rigidly scheduled times, rather than on an as-needed basis. These and other shortcomings of pull-out programs have led to the need for the development of unique service delivery models in gifted education.

As gifted programming changes, the gifted education specialist has new roles and responsibilities. This call for a changing role of the gifted education specialist is well documented throughout the literature (Dettmer, 1993; Hertzog, 1998; Renzulli & Purcell, 1996; Schack, 1996; VanTassel-Baska, 1992). Dettmer called for gifted program teachers to work in new ways, Renzulli and Purcell described expanded roles for the gifted education teacher. Specifically, gifted education teachers need to collaborate with classroom teachers and coordinate curriculum efforts (Hertzog, 1998; Schack, 1996). Gifted education programming must begin to move away from a separate and segregated role to become integrated with the total school program. One service delivery strategy that may bridge these programs is resource consultation and collaboration.

Putting the Research to Use

The study of resource consultation and collaboration as a service delivery model in gifted education has several important implications for best practice in educational programming. First, there are implications for using this approach as a viable service delivery model in gifted education. Second, results have implications for the integration of gifted education for every service delivery approach. Third, implications for including under-represented populations who are seldom formally identified as gifted learners is highlighted in the study findings. Finally, the descriptive data contained in this study provide a compilation of best practices, as well as limitations to using the consultative and collaborative approach to gifted education programming.

The viability of the resource consultation and collaborative model called the Catalyst Program lies in the findings of the study. Enhanced student academic performance, enhanced teacher competencies, and the inclusion of gifted and nongifted students exhibiting gifted behavior provide insight into the effectiveness of the model. The potential for other positive spill-over effects to the total school program further illustrates the viability of this approach for the good of quality education for all students.

Finally, this study outlines the frequency of practices most used to support consultation and collaboration among educators. For example, the practices of coplanning, coteaching, and cluster grouping are illustrated in the data collected in monthly reports and site visitations. The limitations of these practices are highlighted by the non-negotiables that evolved out of data analysis.

Research has shown that general educators want more access to consultant assistance from gifted education specialists and more training and assistance in locating and using appropriate educational materials (Renzulli & Reis, 1994; Tomlinson, Coleman, Allan, Udall, & Landrum, 1996). "If classroom teachers are encouraged to participate actively in the gifted program, they may eventually come to regard efforts to meet the special needs of advanced students as shared responsibility" (Reis, 1983, p. 21). This type of ownership for the gifted program can lead to all educators becoming facilitators to appropriate educational opportunities for all gifted students. It also can result in a greater frequency of services for gifted learners. Further, gifted learners can benefit from having differentiation that extends and enhances the regular curriculum experience because the general educator is participating in the process (Landrum, 1994).

Archambault et al. (1993) suggested that, as gifted education specialists redefine their role from direct services to include more support for classroom teachers, more discussion of the results of these efforts is necessary. Therefore, continued research on the application of resource consultation in gifted education is warranted (see Armstrong, Kirschenbaum, & Landrum, 1999). Hence, a collaborative approach to serving gifted learners, named the Catalyst Program by the school district, was evaluated. In this programming model (see Ward & Landrum, 1994), the gifted education resource role was redefined so that teachers could act as a spark to ignite advocacy and service for gifted learners among general education colleagues (Reid, 1997).

As reported by Armstrong, Kirschenbaum, and Landrum (1999), research in consultation and collaboration in general has been conducted in order to study the effectiveness of models for enhancing student behavior, teacher competencies, and the consultative process (Dettmer, Thurston, & Dyck, 1993). More research is needed in order to duplicate the results of studies from outside the field of gifted education to include all aspects of the consultation process and to replicate initial research conducted on a limited basis in gifted education (Landrum, 1994).

This study was designed to contribute a needed evaluation of resource consultation and collaboration programming in gifted education. The study was directed toward addressing three questions: (1) Will resource consultation enhance student academic performance for gifted learners and their same-age peers? (2) Does resource consultation improve teacher competencies? (3) How effective is the resource consultation process when applied to gifted education?

METHODOLOGY

Participating Sample and Setting

Site. The 10 participating schools were located in the same large, urban school district near a metropolitan area that serves a racially and socioeconomically mixed student population. The school district is the largest in a southeastern state; it has approximately 70 elementary (K-6) school buildings serving 39,000 students, with approximately 17% formally identified as gifted learners. The district was using a pull-out service delivery model that met once a week as a primary service delivery for elementary students in most buildings, although some gifted learners were served at one of four magnet school buildings.

The researcher, a university faculty member serving as consultant to the district, planned the evaluation project. This included developing the resource consultation model implemented within the district, providing pilot schools with staff development through an initial workshop and follow-up site visits, and collecting field notes during site visits. Local gifted education specialists who participated in the pilot project collected student performance data and prepared the monthly consultation activity reports. Other evaluation data were collected by research assistants.

Staff. Participating staff included 6 gifted education teachers assigned to single buildings, 2 itinerant gifted education teachers assigned to two or three school buildings, and 23 general education teachers in grades 2–6 with cluster groups of gifted learners in their classrooms. Each of the 10 elementary schools participating in the pilot project was volunteered by its building administrator.

Students. Thirty-nine gifted students in grades 3–6 who attended one of the 10 pilot project schools were involved in the Catalyst Project. They had been identified as gifted by extremely high scores on standardized group intelligence tests and achievement tests as outlined by state department regulations, or by a problem-solving assessment process based on Gardner's multiple intelligences theory that was conducted each year for all second-grade students. They were matched for age, gender, and socioeconomic status with 53 nongifted students from the same classrooms.

Evaluation Design

School personnel consulted with the researcher to develop a model of resource consultation for gifted learners in their elementary school buildings. The pilot was conducted before deciding where to invest resources in district-wide implementation of the resource consultation or Catalyst model. It was determined that only 10 schools would participate in a pilot of such efforts over a two-year period in order to allow for full implementation of a model in each school building. Further, program outcomes would be assessed in three areas against outcomes demonstrated by resource consultation programs outside the field of gifted education: changes in student behavior, teacher competencies, and effectiveness of the consultation process. Although the evaluation of the pilot project was commissioned for the project, it has important implications for our field that warrant dissemination to a wider audience.

Procedures

The gifted education teacher, general education classroom teachers, administrators, and support personnel (e.g., counselors, media specialists) from each of the pilot schools participated in one-day workshops on collaboration and consultation held at the opening of the school year. Training content consisted of the processes of consultation and collaboration, the model for resource consultation implementation, roles and responsibilities of staff, and collaborative and consultative differentiation of curriculum and instruction. Several follow-up training sessions were conducted throughout the year for each participating school's staff, including district-wide sharing sessions among classroom teachers, monthly after-school staff meetings for gifted education specialists, and building-level in-services on best practices for differentiation.

Training was followed by two years of implementation of a consultation and collaboration model in gifted education. The specific resource consultation model implemented in this evaluation was developed by Curtis, Curtis, and Graden (1988) and adapted for gifted education by Ward and Landrum (1994). According to the Ward and Landrum model, consultation for student-related problems can occur at different levels. This model allows for filtering cases through each level of the hierarchy. At level one, teachers seek to collaborate with other teachers on an unstructured, informal basis. Classroom teachers seek assistance from specialized gifted education personnel at level two of the model. Level three represents team intervention with several staff members affected by decision making.

Data Collection

Data collection included student academic performance on a standardized test of cognitive processes conducted in the first two months of year one and in the month of May during year two, general education classroom teacher observations using an established protocol, and monthly consultation activity reports collected by gifted education specialists and developed by the researcher. In addition, field notes consisting of a priori categories were consistently recorded by the researcher during all site visits to the pilot schools across two years.

Enhanced student academic performance for gifted learners and their same-age peers. Student achievement was assessed using the Ross Test for Higher Cognitive Processes (Ross & Ross, 1976) because most goals of differentiated educational opportunities in gifted education include improved higher order thinking. This test provides normative scoring data for both gifted learners alone (IQ of at least 125 on a standardized intelligence test) and gifted and nongifted student populations combined from regular classrooms in grades 4–6. Gifted and nongifted students were tested at the beginning of the first year of the pilot project and at the end of the second year of the pilot (except for one school that was added in year two).

Improved teacher competencies. Evidence of specific instructional practices supportive of gifted learners that had been implemented by teachers were collected in pre- and postassessments during the first and second years respectively in independent classroom observations of at least 45 minutes. Three independent raters used the Classroom Practices Record (CPR; Westberg, Dobyns, & Archambault, 1993) to conduct these assessments. The CPR was used to document the differentiated instruction that gifted and talented students received through classroom activities, instructional materials, and verbal interactions. The instrument contains six sections: identification information, physical environment inventory, curricular activities, verbal interactions, teacher interview record, and daily summary. It has an inter-rater reliability of .85.

The effectiveness of the consulting process applied to gifted education. Issues important to understanding the resource consultation process in gifted education included (a) the role of the gifted education specialist and (b) the time-efficiency and cost-effectiveness of these efforts.

The nature of the roles was indicated by teachers' acknowledgement of the frequency and type of activity in which they were engaged. The nature of the role expansion of the gifted education specialist was assessed by examining descriptive statistics on the data collected on monthly staff activity reports of the specialists' direct and indirect service delivery of differentiated instructional practices for gifted learners. An increase of indirect services indicates a redefinition of the traditional role of direct service for the gifted education specialist. All gifted education specialists were instructed to move from their traditionally

Table I   Mean Group Scores for Higher Cognitive Processes for Gifted (n = 39) and Nongifted Learners (n = 53)

Subtest	Gifted Students					Nongifted Students				
	Pretest		Posttest			Pretest		Posttest		
	M	SD	M	SD	t	M	SD	M	SD	t
Abstract Relations	80.17	(29.48)	88.17	(26.25)		95.80	(10.16)	99.00	(15.53)	
Analogies	98.46	(23.19)	102.85	(15.69)		108.72	(14.60)	120.18	(14.70)	
Analysis Subtest	90.69	(26.78)	100.90	(18.12)		106.00	(9.99)	111.33	(12.24)	
Analysis of Attributes	94.81	(15.14)	99.04	(17.30)		105.46	(14.89)	108.03	(16.87)	
Deductive Reasoning	90.12	(19.47)	95.94	(15.38)		106.72	(12.03)	107.59	(15.31)	
Evaluation Subtest	97.33	(16.69)	102.00	(11.71)		110.03	(9.96)	112.49	(10.65)	
Analysis of Information	99.06	(18.44)	104.39	(13.50)		107.90	(14.85)	109.64	(16.78)	
Missing Premises	87.93	(25.45)	101.74	(17.59)		101.44	(11.98)	106.69	(16.09)	
Questioning Strategies	105.33	(13.42)	106.38	(14.27)		112.51	(12.25)	118.03	(9.18)	
Sequential Synthesis	98.14	(18.69)	107.50	(20.39)		105.74	(15.68)	105.10	(19.45)	
Synthesis Subtest	85.29	(23.48)	97.40	(18.28)		102.21	(9.72)	105.00	(12.91)	
Total Score	88.88	(24.16)	102.10	(15.46)	3.80*	103.71	(11.76)	113.00	(13.39)	2.03**

Note. Separate normative samples are used for the standardization of the scores for gifted and nongifted students.
*$p < .001$, **$p < .05$

totally direct service delivery approach to indirect service delivery as much as possible and to preserve direct services for those activities not deemed appropriate for indirect service delivery. No specified percentages of time in either direct or indirect service delivery mode was specified by the consultant, nor were expectations set by the school district on this issue.

The effectiveness and efficiency of resource consultation and collaboration were assessed by collecting frequency data on monthly activity reports (a maximum of nine for each school per year) by the gifted education specialist. Specifically, the report recorded the frequency and duration of consultation and collaboration activities such as team teaching and shared planning, the target audiences for service delivery, and the use of resources in consultation and collaboration activities. The frequencies of services delivered were recorded on these reports as well, along with other related activities.

Data extracted from monthly reports denoted the frequency and duration of collaborative activities. Specifically, the reports recorded the frequency of consultation activities, including lesson development and implementation, materials development and organization, and the nature of conferencing. The number and nature of student audiences and teachers involved in lessons were also recorded on the monthly reports. Anecdotal data from the field notes collected by the project consultant upon site visits to pilot schools enhanced the descriptive data.

Data Analysis

In order to investigate differences among scores on student academic performance for the treatment and control groups, paired independent t-tests were performed on mean pre- and posttest total scores for the Ross Test of Critical Thinking (Ross & Ross, 1976). Descriptive summaries of pre- and postassessments of independent observations of classroom environments were prepared for a random sample of classroom teachers using the Classroom Practices Record (Westberg, Dobyns, & Archambault, 1993). In order to determine the nature of the consulting process in the context of gifted education, descriptive statistics of the frequency and duration of consultative activities were compiled on separate items in teachers' monthly reports, including collaborative teaching, planning sessions, types of materials used, and so forth. Descriptive statistics on demographic data such as number of students served and the composition of student groups during lessons were also recorded on monthly reports. Anecdotal information from onsite visitations was gleaned from field notes. A priori categories of trends among consultative lessons emerged over initial sets of field notes and were consistently used to guide the content of field notes throughout the two years.

RESULTS

Results were analyzed in three areas: enhanced student academic performance, improved teacher competencies, and understanding of the nature of the consulting process in gifted education.

Enhanced Student Academic Performance

Student academic performance was measured by assessing higher order cognitive thinking using the Ross Test of Higher Cognitive Processes in pre- and posttests (Ross & Ross, 1976). The test was given to identify gifted students and nongifted students in target classrooms. The independent ratings of student higher cognitive processing resulted in significantly increased mean composite or total scores for both gifted (from $M = 88.88$ to $M = 102.10$; $t = 3.80$, $p < .001$) and participating nongifted (from $M = 103.71$ to $M = 113.00$; $t = 2.03$, $p < .05$) students from pre- to postassessments (see Table 1). Note that means for gifted and nongifted students on this instrument are standardized differently, using two different comparative samples. The gifted education sample includes students with intelligence scores of 125 or higher, while the nongifted sample includes students with scores of 124 or lower. The scores for each sample are relative to different expectations for the same number correct in the standardization of the group and, therefore, cannot be compared directly with one another.

It is noteworthy here that each group score was significantly higher in the postassessment, and that the increase for the gifted group was greater than the gains made by the nongifted group. This is evidence of enhanced academic performance for all students, with slightly more benefit to gifted learners.

Although the frequency of differentiated lessons and the number of participating students engaged in them is no guarantee of successful academic

Table 2   Frequency of Differentiated Lessons Taught by Type (Year 1 N = 63, Year 2 N = 81)

Type of Differentiated Lesson	Year 1		Year 2	
	Frequency	(%)	Frequency	(%)
Original lesson	44	(23%)	47	(20%)
Collaboration lessons	38	(19%)	47	(20%)
Demonstration lessons	31	(16%)	32	(14%)
Pull-out lessons	46	(24%)	49	(21%)
Regular classroom observations	13	(6%)	20	(9%)
Team-taught lessons	23	(12%)	38	(16%)
Total	195	(100%)	233	(100%)

Note. Frequencies represent times noted on monthly reports. During year two, several schools lost their sixth-grade classes to the middle school, thus decreasing the total student population that might have been served.

performance, it does open the possibility for enhanced academic rigor for all participating students. According to the monthly reports of consultation activity at 10 schools, teachers implemented an average of 195 differentiated lessons to students in year one and 233 such lessons in year two (see Table 2). In the traditional pull-out program that existed in the school district, identified students participated in differentiated lessons no more than once or twice a week for an average of two hours, or considerably fewer lessons than students are provided through consultation. Monthly records also included data indicating that approximately 1,215 identified gifted learners were provided differentiated instruction through consulting efforts during the first year of the pilot project, while 1,132 gifted learners were served in year two. During the first year of the pilot project, approximately 1,032 nongifted learners participated in differentiated lessons, while 994 similar students participated in year two (see Table 3). This decrease in students served was most likely due to the move of the sixth graders from the elementary schools to the middle schools between years one and two. Customarily, gifted education programs do not include nongifted learners; however, in the consulting model, nongifted students participated in differentiated lessons when they demonstrated educational needs similar to that of gifted learners. Thus, nongifted learners had educational opportunities from which they might otherwise have been excluded if those services were not provided via consultation and collaboration with general educators.

The field notes from site visits elaborate on the nature of instructional materials used during differentiated lessons. This may indicate something positive about the quality of the academic experiences of the students, which might lead to enhanced academic performance. In particular, the advanced, complex, and sophisticated nature of differentiated experiences create differentiated learning experiences. For example, the specialist provided guest speakers, research

Table 3   Frequency of Gifted and Nongifted Students Served by Resource Consultation and Collaboration (Year 1 N = 63, Year 2 N = 81)

Size of Student Group Served	Gifted		Nongifted	
	Year 1 Frequency	Year 2 Frequency	Year 1 Frequency	Year 2 Frequency
1–5	15	5	14	6
6–10	18	6	16	5
11–15	15	11	5	6
16–20	3	2	5	5
21–24	0	8	3	1
25+	27	26	23	28
Other	11	11	7	12

Note. Frequencies represent times noted on monthly reports. During year two, several schools lost their sixth-grade classes to the middle school, thus decreasing the total student population that might have been served.

materials, novels to replace basal readers, and laboratory equipment to general education classroom teachers. These materials came from classrooms at advanced levels, libraries, community resources, or gifted education sources. They provided classroom teachers with the appropriate curricular and instructional tools to provide differentiated learning experiences to high-ability learners.

Field notes of the project consultant also included additional indicators about the opportunity for enhanced student academic performance for gifted and nongifted learners who participated in differentiated lessons. Provisions for gifted learners included monitored continuous progress through the provision of grades for most differentiated lessons, the development of appropriate rubrics for student performance evaluation, and the practice of the preassessment of students prior to placement in instructional activities. Further, differentiated lessons included multiple instructors who brought together different expertise in designing and implementing lessons to challenge students academically.

Improved Teacher Competencies

The Classroom Practices Record (Westberg, Dobyns, & Archambault, 1993), pre- and postassessment of teacher behavior, was used to assess changes in teachers' competencies in differentiating instructional practices for gifted learners. Initial classroom observations (N = 7) indicated that teachers most frequently lectured and explained information (23%) and assigned written work (23%) to students during classroom lessons, thus indicating poor competency overall for appropriately differentiating instruction (see Table 4). This is particularly problematic given that about half of the classrooms (48%) were heterogeneous, which implies that students in the same classroom participated in whole-group instruction in spite of extreme variances in ability present in the same classroom. Most of the verbal interactions that took place among students and teachers involved responding to teachers' questions (31%), explaining and making statements (26%), and making requests or commands while requiring students' use of higher order thinking infrequently (11%). No differentiation occurred in 57% of the preassessment lessons.

The postassessment classroom observations ($N = 17$) pointed to more frequently differentiated instructional practices, demonstrating an improvement in teacher competencies during the lessons observed (see Table 4). Although the most prevalent curricular activity remained explanation and lecture (23%), many more varied curricular activities, including those that differentiate instruction, were noted. Observers noted an increase in the use of independent study (18%) and a variety of other differentiation strategies (12%). Student grouping for instruction was largely whole group (60%), while the composition of the group was almost always (84%) homogeneous, typically high-level learners. It is important to note that individualization (16%) was evident in some lessons, even among homogeneous classrooms. Some small-(14%) and large-group (10%) lessons were also evident. There were subtle changes in classroom verbal interactions. For example, there was an increase in questioning (34%) and wait time following (26%) all questions. Some differentiation was seen in modifications of lesson content (32%), process (22%), and product (16%). Although this might seem like a decrease from preassessments at first sight, remember there were larger numbers of differentiated lessons observed during the second assessment. Finally, and perhaps most importantly, there was a substantial decrease in lessons without differentiation (6%) during postassessments.

The Classroom Practices Record includes an interview protocol for teachers to be used following a classroom observation. Teachers respond to questions about the nature of curricular and instructional differentiation, as well as decision making regarding student grouping. Interviews indicated that three of the seven teachers in the initial observations indicated no intent for curricular and instructional differentiation in the lesson. The other four classroom teachers indicated using advanced student novels, group discussion, questioning, problem solving, and allowing students to work at their own pace as a means of differentiation. Teachers reported instructional grouping as whole group in heterogeneous classrooms with gifted learners as a cluster group in the classroom. Finally, teachers indicated that they determined student grouping by level of mastery and test scores.

During the postassessment interviews, responses indicated frequent and varied differentiation of curriculum and instruction, as well as varied practices for grouping students. In addition to those differentiation strategies employed in preassessments, teachers indicated that they use the following differentiation practices: varying entry/exit points for mastery learning, student choice of work product, learning stations, contracts, advanced content, individualized student assignments, higher order thinking skills, field experiences, same-ability

Table 4   Pre- and Postobservations of General Education Classroom Instructional Practices Using the Classroom Practices Record (Year 1 N = 7, Year 2 N = 17)

Type of Classroom Practice	Year 1 Percentage	Year 2 Percentage
Curricular Activities		
Audio visual	8%	0%
Demonstration	8%	12%
Discussion	19%	16%
Explanation/Lecture	23%	23%
Games	0%	2%
Nonacademic	3%	3%
Oral reading	4%	3%
Project work	0%	9%
Review/recitation	8%	12%
Silent reading	4%	0%
Simulation/role play	0%	3%
Testing	0%	2%
Verbal practice	0%	3%
Written assignments	23%	12%
Grouping Size		
Individually	19%	16%
Small group	27%	14%
Large group	19%	10%
Total class	35%	60%
Group Composition		
Homogeneous	52%	84%
Heterogeneous	48%	16%
Verbal Interaction		
Knowledge/comprehension questions	(13%)	(21%)
Higher order thinking questions	(11%)	(13%)
Request or command	(19%)	(21%)
Explanation/statement	(26%)	(27%)
Response	(31%)	(8%)
No verbal response	0	(1%)
Wait Time	**2 (4%)**	**35 (26%)**
Types of Learning Centers		
3 or more	(43%)	(50%)
2 or more	(43%)	(22%)
1	0	(17%)
None	(14%)	(11%)
Differentiation Strategies		
Advanced content	(40%)	(32%)
Advanced process	(30%)	(22%)
Advanced product	0	(16%)
Independent study (assigned)	0	(12%)
Independent study (self-selected)	0	(6%)
Other differentiation	0	(12%)
No differentiation	4 (57.14%)	1 (5.88%)

Note. The participating classrooms contained 21-30 children and were third- or fourth-grade classrooms. Wait time reflects total number of questions observed in pre- and postsessions. No differentiation data reflect the total number of lessons in both pre- and postobservations.

peer interactions, coteaching, and differentiated student work product rubrics. Similarly, teachers named a greater number and variety of reasons used to make instructional grouping decisions. When asked what specific grouping formats they used, teachers indicated that they used any number of the following: self-contained homogeneous, multiage teams and cluster grouping. Although some student grouping was still determined by performance on tests, teachers also indicated using preassessments, portfolios, and curriculum-based assessments.

The field notes of the project consultant included observations that recognize the shared responsibility for the education of gifted learners among gifted education specialists and members of school staffs. This shared responsibility represents new teacher competencies for all participating staff. The classroom teacher participated in planning differentiated lessons, while the gifted education specialist conducted on-going student assessments of differentiated work products. For both groups of teachers, this signifies new teacher behaviors or competencies. Other examples of shared responsibility included determining student grouping for instruction, the preparation and delivery of differentiated lessons, and regularly scheduled coplanning.

The Effectiveness of the Consulting Process

Time efficiency is illustrated by the distribution of time expended by the gifted education teacher (see Table 5). The efficiency of time is related to the amount of differentiation that can be provided to as many students as possible. In this case, it means how much indirect or collaborative service can be implemented, given that indirect services employ the expertise of several persons and are provided to students whenever needed through the regular classroom. During the two years of the pilot, the specialists spent 67% and 64% of the time respectively in each year of the pilot involved in indirect activity and only 33% and 36% in direct service delivery. *Indirect service delivery* refers to activities that involved collaboration and consultation, while direct service delivery involved the individual efforts of the gifted education specialist. Further analysis (see Table 6) also indicates the distribution of time for daily activities. The 195 and 233 (see Table 2) differentiated lessons provided to students in years one and two respectively accounted for 40% and 41% of the total activity of the specialists. Another 22% and 26% of their time was spent gathering and preparing materials for instruction in the first and second years. Clearly, the majority of their activity was used in instructional preparation and implementation (62% and 67% respectively).

Other indicators of time efficiency are revealed in the analysis of gifted education specialists' distribution of time consulting (see Table 7) with one another as measured by the frequency of time spent making initial contacts, planning, lesson implementation, and follow-up. For example, from year one (17%) to two (31%), gifted education specialists spent nearly double the amount of time making initial contact with colleagues in intervals as brief as 1–15 minutes. Planning time became more efficient as staffs made increasingly greater use in years one (63%) and two (84%) of weekly planning time of less than an hour.

Table 5   Distribution of Indirect and Direct Service Delivery for Gifted Education Specialists (Year 1 N = 63, Year 2 N = 81)

Service Delivery Activity	Indirect Service Delivery		Direct Service Delivery	
	Year 1	Year 2	Year 1	Year 2
	Frequency		Frequency	
Original lesson			44	47
Demonstration lesson			31	32
Pull-out lesson			46	49
Regular classroom observation			13	20
Total			134 (33%)	148 (36%)
Initial contact	65	78		
Planning sessions	80	50		
Follow-up sessions	67	51		
Collaboration lesson	38	47		
Team-taught lesson	23	38		
Total	273 (67%)	264 (64%)		

Note. Frequencies represent times noted on monthly reports. During year two, several schools lost their sixth-grade classes to the middle school, thus decreasing the total student population that might have been served.

Table 6   Distribution of the Gifted Education Specialists' Time Spent in Daily Activities Related to Collaboration and Consultation (Year 1 N = 63, Year 2 N = 81)

Type of Catalyst Teacher Activity	Year 1		Year 2	
	Freq.	%	Freq.	%
Student Identification	90	(18%)	110	(19%)
Conferences	96	(20%)	78	(14%)
Lessons (Instructional Time)	195	(40%)	233	(41%)
Materials Development/Distribution	106	(22%)	145	(26%)

Note. Frequencies represent times noted on monthly reports. During year two, several schools lost their sixth-grade classes to the middle school, thus decreasing the total student population that might have been served.

Implementation of lessons or instructional time, however, was greater than half an hour and up to two hours per lesson of the time in year one (71%) and in year two (65%). Follow-up was consistent over two years with 73% and 71% of the time kept brief at under one hour. Therefore, the greatest length of time that educators spent together consulting involved instructional time.

Table 7   Distribution of the Gifted Education Specialists' Time Spent with Educators Who Participated in Resource Consultation and Collaboration for Gifted Education (Year 1 N = 63, Year 2 N = 81)

Time in Resource Consultation	Year 1		Year 2	
	Freq.	%	Freq.	%
Initial contact	65	(23%)	78	(27%)
Planning sessions	80	(28%)	50	(24%)
Implementation (instruction)	76	(26%)	69	(28%)
Follow-up sessions	67	(23%)	51	(21%)

Note. Frequencies represent the number of times each activity was noted on monthly reports. During year two, several schools lost their sixth-grade classes to the middle school, thus decreasing the total student population that might have been served.

A basic premise of the consulting approach is that the gifted education specialist can work with classroom teachers and other educators to provide differentiation in the general classroom, even as they reduce the number of direct services that they provide. Through consultation and collaboration, the gifted education specialist in this project worked with teachers, support staff, administrators, and others. A distribution of time spent with others indicates that the specialist spent more time with individual teachers (see Table 8) from year one (10%) to year two (25%), resulting in an increase in collaborative partnerships over time. Differentiated lessons available through the consulting approach are provided by an increased number of teachers and instructional specialists, thereby making service delivery more cost-effective. Given that in years one and two of the pilot respectively, the gifted education specialists worked with grade-level teachers or small groups of teachers rather than individuals 63% and 47% of the time, their time expended in collaborating and consulting was efficient. Further, these results illustrate the efficiency of the consultative service delivery model over time.

An analysis of the ratio of gifted education specialists to students served and faculty with whom they collaborated indicates the distribution of gifted education specialists' time and energy across classrooms and students. In this pilot project, all gifted students and nongifted students with high ability were cluster grouped in classrooms targeted for collaboration. The level of activity reported here is consistent with a specific ratio of 1 specialist to 9–12 teachers and 1 gifted education specialist to 120 students.

Redefinition of role of the gifted education specialist. An examination of the monthly reports compiled by the gifted education teacher chronicled the shift away from the traditional gifted education specialist to a redefined role. The greatest

Table 8   Distribution of Nature of Teacher Group Involved in Collaboration with Gifted Education Specialists (Year 1 N = 63, Year 2 N = 81)

Nature of Teachers Involved in Collaboration	Year 1		Year 2	
	Freq.	%	Freq.	%
Individual	10	(10%)	27	(25%)
Grade-Level Teachers	31	(29%)	25	(24%)
Two or More Teachers	35	(33%)	25	(24%)
Problem-Solving Group	1	(1%)	1	(1%)
Support Staff	3	(3%)	10	(9%)
Administrators	10	(10%)	6	(6%)
Others	15	(14%)	12	(11%)

Note. Frequencies represent times noted on monthly reports. During year two, several schools lost their sixth-grade classes to the middle school, thus decreasing the total student population that might have been served.

influence on the redefinition of the role of the gifted education specialist was the nature of the consultative service delivery. Gifted education specialists spent 67% of their total provisions of instructional services in the first year and 64% of their time during the second year in indirect services (see Table 5). Indirect services are differentiated provisions for students that are prepared and delivered collaboratively with general education, including collaborative (coplanned) lessons, coteaching lessons, initial contact with colleagues who need services, coplanning, and follow-up. Direct services are differentiated provisions for students that are the sole responsibility of the gifted education specialist. Gifted education specialists spent 33% and 36% of their time in years one and two respectively in direct services. The inclusion and dominance of indirect services in the collaborative experience redesigned the role of the gifted education specialist from a predominantly direct service delivery model.

The data collected on 63 monthly reports from year one and 81 monthly reports from year two that show the distribution of instructional time spent in the consulting and collaborative approach help define the role of the gifted education specialist during the pilot project (see Table 2). The most prominent instructional activity of the gifted education specialist was implementing original pull-out lessons as an extension of the regular education curricula. In year one, the gifted education specialist spent 24% of instructional time in pull-out lessons and 21% during year two. This reinforces the importance of retaining the gifted education specialist in any service delivery model in order to provide differentiated learning opportunities. However, the role of the gifted education specialist has changed to include indirect or collaborative lessons. Across the two years, the specialist consistently spent nearly equal amounts of time developing new lessons and implementing collaborative lessons. Team-teaching

Table 9   Distribution of the Gifted Education Specialists' Time Spent on Instructional Activities Preparation and Implementation (Year 1 N = 63, Year 2 N = 81)

Type of Instructional Activity	Year 1		Year 2	
	Freq.	%	Freq.	%
Preparation of pull-out lesson materials	39	(37%)	50	(35%)
Preparation of original lesson materials	35	(33%)	44	(30%)
Dissemination of resources/information	20	(19%)	41	(28%)
Provision of training on use of materials	12	(11%)	10	(7%)

Note. Frequencies represent times noted on monthly reports. During year two, several schools lost their sixth-grade classes to the middle school, thus decreasing the total student population that might have been served.

increased from 12% to 16% over the two years. Smaller amounts of time were consistently spent conducting observations of classrooms and demonstration lessons that were minimally gifted education collaboration activities.

Teachers spent time preparing instructional materials in various ways (see Table 9). The gifted education specialist developed pull-out materials for instruction (37% and 35% in years one and two respectively). Similarly, in years one and two, 33% and 30% of the materials were original materials that they created on their own. The specialists also disseminated resources to general education teachers. Therefore, in the first year 19% and in the second year 28% of the materials were developed for indirect services. This increase shows that specialists were able to develop significantly more materials for teachers over time.

Context of consultation activities. The consultative and collaborative activities documented in field notes during site visits included coplanning, coteaching, providing differentiated educational opportunities, linking gifted and general education curricula, sharing responsibility for student assessment, and gathering and distributing educational resources. School staffs met on a regular basis to collaboratively plan for differentiated educational opportunities for gifted learners, which led to the linking of general education and gifted education curricula. In other words, modifications were made to the general education curricula in order to develop differentiated curricula and instructional practices for gifted learners. Coplanning sessions ranged in frequency and duration across grade levels and buildings. Planning time occurred minimally once a week and as frequently as twice a week, lasting from 30 minutes to 1 ½ hours per session. The sessions were conducted with a single classroom teacher and the gifted education specialist, with several teachers and specialists together, or with the specialist and a given set of teachers at the same grade level. The purposes of the sessions included planning for collaborative teaching, follow-up, and student assessment.

In addition to coplanning, teachers delivered instruction together. Coteaching efforts involved team teaching, demonstration teaching, providing supportive learning activities, and complementary teaching. All types of coteaching were evidenced across schools. The demonstration lessons involved having the gifted education specialist prepare differentiated lessons for the entire heterogeneous classroom in order to stimulate high interest and high ability in any student. The intent was to involve the classroom teacher in some aspect of the lesson or to observe student behavior in response to the lesson. Although very limited, some general education staff and support personnel worked together on specific follow-up collaborative activities after having worked with the gifted education specialist. Again, on a limited basis, the gifted education specialist facilitated team problem-solving sessions among school staff regarding problems or concerns associated with the provision of differentiated education for gifted learners.

The means by which school staffs collaborated in the provision of differentiated educational activities were varied. Some of the instructional strategies included the use of contracts, independent study, the use of higher order thinking skills, compacting, tiered assignments, a problems-based approach, and research. Strategies used to differentiate curricula included advanced content, acceleration into advanced classrooms, use of supplemental curricula, problem-solving programs, and the development of original curricula. The most unique characteristic of the collaborative lessons was that they reflected an integration of general and gifted education programs. Differentiated lessons were based on extending or increasing the depth of the general education curriculum. This integration provided a common understanding among all school staff about the educational experiences of gifted learners. Further, it offered students a bridge between programs to facilitate a transfer of learning.

Anecdotal information from the consultant's field notes indicate the presence of barriers or impediments to the consulting process. For example, competing school reforms inhibited the comprehensiveness and fluency of the collaborative and consultative approaches (e.g., the abolishment of homogeneous grouping, standards movement, and emphasis on competency and proficiency testing). Turnover of staff from year to year resulted in the need for repeating staff development and for "jump-starting" the program with new staff members. It follows that, when staff development for the model was not provided, the service delivery model was either never initiated or was extremely limited in scope. Obviously, when no staff development was conducted for a school participating in the collaboration, success was limited. The excessive number of schools, teachers, or students with whom any one gifted education specialist worked restricted the program outcomes. Without the flexible grouping of students, consultation and collaboration efforts were extremely limited in frequency and duration. Teachers who were not given a common planning time also were unable to initiate or maintain collaborative activity. Administrative support was critical for the validity and credibility of the program with staff. Finally, staff members who were not participating in the collaborative process on a volunteer basis were not likely to participate in differentiated lessons frequently or at all.

EDUCATIONAL IMPLICATIONS

Overall, the resource consultation model led to diverse and more frequent services to gifted learners, resulting in the provision of differentiated education to gifted students. Educational services provided to both gifted and nongifted students in the general education classroom were enhanced by the use of a variety of effective instructional practices by general classroom teachers, and more specialized services were made accessible to unidentified students. With the use of resource consultation, there was a steady increase over time in the frequency of services provided to gifted and nongifted students.

The findings of this pilot project demonstrate how resource consultation moves differentiated education for gifted learners and nonidentified participants away from the exclusive provision of services outside of the general education classroom to a model that includes the provision of services both inside and outside of the general education program. The frequency and diversity of student services were enhanced when compared to the services provided gifted students through traditional educational models. Further, the frequency of instructional time in differentiated lessons was increased. Each instructional lesson was from one to two hours long. Clearly, these findings demonstrate the expansion of services for gifted learners along with the inclusion of more students in services (gifted and nongifted learners) without an increase of specialized personnel, which would require additional funding because the gifted education program embraced the participation of classroom teachers and other personnel in the resource consultation service delivery model.

The potential positive spill-over effects for the entire school and district that emerged from the implementation of consultative and collaborative efforts were an important outcome of this pilot project. For instance, there was enhanced professional development for the entire staff of each school. Gifted education specialists learned more about the general education program, while classroom teachers and other specialists became more familiar with the field of gifted education. Not only did educators benefit from this process, but students not formally identified as gifted demonstrated gains from these services. There were other positive effects for students, as well. Occasionally, students participated in differentiated lessons inside and outside of the regular classroom when they were able to demonstrate requisite mastery levels of the regular curriculum. The students who were left in the regular classroom had a smaller teacher-to-student ratio. In a traditional gifted education program, these students would not have been given opportunities to demonstrate the abilities or participate in differentiated lessons. All in all, schools developed a culture of shared responsibility and a collaborative atmosphere.

Further, the inclusion of students not typically identified as gifted had several benefits for the gifted program. First, this approach made student services appear less elitist, which has been a common criticism of gifted programs. Second, students who were gifted but eluded identification freely participated in the provision of differentiated lessons, thus improving the likelihood of being identified as gifted in the future. For example, many teachers reported observing behaviors in students during a demonstration lesson or other differentiated lesson in their classrooms that they had not seen previously. Such observations can lead to the referral of children for gifted education services and inclusion in target collaborative classrooms in the future. Formal identification remained critical because of state mandates requiring the process at local levels and because the differentiated needs of students without labels may go undetected by some teachers.

Finally, resource consultation appeared to be an effective and efficient way to provide differentiated education to gifted learners. The findings suggest that resource consultation may have served to enhance the school system's potential to serve the differentiated needs of gifted students. Moreover, increased teacher skills in using differentiated curricular and instructional practices should be beneficial for all students, as improved services to nongifted students through direct instruction and overall improved teacher instructional competence offer the potential for spill-over effects. These effects may help bridge gifted and general education programs, as well as provide otherwise unavailable resources to some students.

A review of the literature on consulting highlights the typical pitfalls and perils of consulting (Huefner, 1988; Johnson, Pugach, & Hamilton, 1988). Dettmer, Thurston, and Dyck (1993) reorganized the most significant obstacles into four groups: lack of role definition; absence of a framework within which to consult; failure to document and evaluate both formal and informal consultation and collaboration; and little or no training in consultation skills. These barriers are predictable and were obvious in the pilot project reported here. The identification of specific impediments to the consulting process allow for the recognition of the most important and requisite components of the process. They are non-negotiable components of resource consultation:

1. flexible pacing of instruction;

2. flexible student grouping, including pull-out;

3. regularly scheduled planning time (short and long term);

4. voluntary participation;

5. staff development;

6. administrative support (advocacy, validation, and maintenance);

7. documentation of consultation activities;

8. low ratio of gifted education specialists to number of colleagues involved in collaborative efforts;

9. participation of gifted education specialists with expertise in the field; and

10. continuation of support for direct service delivery for gifted learners by trained specialist.

Special Issues for Gifted Education

There is a concern among some professional educators that gifted education services may become watered down or eliminated altogether when gifted learners are served exclusively in the general education classroom environment. Indeed, many differentiated programs for gifted learners are based on the notion that the general education classroom is not conducive to the unique academic and socioemotional needs of gifted learners; thus, resource consultation may also be viewed with skepticism. The educational advantages for the gifted learner noted in these findings, however, may serve to diminish concerns about gifted education services becoming watered down in the general education classroom. In fact, the frequency and diversity of student services were enhanced when compared to the services offered gifted students through traditional educational models. Of course, assessment of the quality experiences in this service delivery model is as important an issue as any other approach. Unfortunately, this study did not involve a comparison of the two approaches at any level.

The continued need for pull-out lessons regardless of the inclusion of more staff involvement and the inclusion of indirect services for gifted learners was evident in the findings of this evaluation. Although the frequency of services to gifted learners increased, primarily through collaborative efforts, there was still an ongoing request for pull-out services. The frequency of pull-out lessons decreased substantially from earlier service delivery models; but, nonetheless, it was necessary at some level. In fact, most of the differentiation that took place in this pilot project was the responsibility of the gifted education specialist, either singularly or in collaboration with others. Pull-out services were employed when absolutely necessary and after having ruled out collaborative efforts. Thus, pull-out services had greater purpose than before. These findings are as much an assurance that there is a need for a gifted education specialist in any provisions for differentiated gifted learners as it is an assurance that without collaborative efforts, general classroom differentiation is nearly nonexistent.

Finally, the role of the gifted education teacher was transformed as a result of collaboration and consultation. The gifted education teacher model moved away from being the once isolated person who was often singularly responsible for providing differentiated services to one who offered a combination of direct and indirect services. Comparisons of this model to other approaches, such as special classes, is warranted in the future.

The findings of this evaluation illustrate the redefined role of the gifted education teacher as that of a gifted education specialist who serves as a catalyst

(Reid, 1997) among the school staff for providing alternative or differentiated educational experiences to those students who most need them. Therefore, the gifted education specialist shared responsibility for the differentiated education of gifted learners with participating school staff members who engaged in collaborative efforts.

Limitations and Future Directions

Several limitations to the evaluation must be addressed to interpret fully the outcomes and to conduct future research. First, the diverse roles played by the author (e.g., consultant, staff developer, and evaluator) contributed to the significance of the findings. Further, certain aspects of the data collection must be addressed to enhance the impact of the findings. For example, academic performance was only assessed with the Ross Cognitive Ability Test and should include a variety of measures. The quality, rather than just the quantity, of the academic opportunities provided to students through resource consultation must be determined. Then, too, potential spill-over effects for the entire school that have been implied in the findings reported here must be validated. Finally, a very important limitation of any single pilot project is that ensuing findings are specific to the contextual circumstances of the one application. In this study, the distribution of specialized staff to school staff and students would be relevant only to this specific situation.

Future research can be enhanced from a close look at the evaluation findings discussed above and the limitations of the evaluation that produced them. Further research in this area might make use of an experimental design that would add to the rigor of subsequent findings. In particular, the design might be set up to collect preliminary data regarding the existing service delivery model (e.g., frequency and duration of services, quality of services, number of students served, etc.) or data might be collected concurrently with the use of a control. Regardless of the research design imposed, any future studies must include expanded data sources for assessing student academic performance and the quality of differentiated services developed. Further, the overall effects on the entire school (e.g., benefits of staff development, cluster grouping, reduction of students participating in regular education lessons, etc.) should be assessed fully.

The findings from this pilot project are based on a definitive ratio of specialists to staff and students. It seems that these findings would be challenged under circumstances where this ratio is greater. Given the diversity of gifted and talented programs and staffs across the country, this would be important in determining the impact of this service delivery model on a variety of school settings. Finally, an outside researcher who does not serve dual roles in the process—a consultant for example—would lend greater credibility to the findings.

REFERENCES

Archambault, F. X., Westberg, K. L., Brown, S. W., Hallmark, B. W., Zhang, W., & Emons, C. L. (1993). Classroom practices used with gifted third- and fourth-grade students. *Journal for the Education of the Gifted, 16,* 103–119.

Armstrong, D., Kirschenbaum, R., & Landrum, M. S. (1999). The resource consultation model in gifted education to support talent development in today's inclusive schools. *Gifted Child Quarterly, 43,* 39–47.

Curtis, M. J., Curtis, V. A., & Graden, J. L. (1988). Prevention and early intervention assistance programs. *School Psychology International, 9,* 257–264.

Dettmer, P. (1993). Gifted education: Window of opportunity. *Gifted Child Quarterly, 27,* 92–97.

Dettmer, P., Thurston, L., & Dyck, N. (1993). *Consultation, collaboration, and teamwork for students with special needs.* Boston: Allyn and Bacon.

Hertzog, N. B. (1998, January/February). The changing role of the gifted education specialist. *Teaching Exceptional Children 30,* 39–43.

Huefner, D. S. (1988). The consulting teacher model: Risks and opportunities. *Exceptional Children, 54,* 403–414.

Johnson, L. J., Pugach, M. C., & Hamilton, D. (1988). Barriers to effective special education consultation. *Remedial and Special Education, 9*(6), 41–47.

Landrum, M. S. (1994, April). *A study of the nature of effective resource consultation in the education of the gifted.* Paper presented at the annual meeting of the American Educational Research Association, New Orleans, LA.

Reid, C. (1997). *Vision 2000.* Charlotte, NC: Charlotte-Mecklenburg Public Schools.

Reis, S. M. (1983). Creating ownership in gifted and talented programs. *Roeper Review, 5*(4), 20–23.

Renzulli, J. S., & Purcell, J. H. (1996). Gifted education: A look around and a look ahead. *Roeper Review,18,* 173–178.

Renzulli, J. S., & Reis, S. M. (1994). Research related to the schoolwide enrichment triad model. *Gifted Child Quarterly, 38,* 7–20.

Ross, J. D., & Ross, C. M. (1976). *The Ross test of higher cognitive processes.* Novato, CA: Academic Therapy Publications.

Schack, G. D. (1996). All aboard or standing on the shore? Gifted education and the educational reform movement. *Roeper Review, 18,* 190–197.

Tomlinson, C. A., Coleman, M. R., Allan, S., Udall, A., & Landrum, M. (1996). Interface between gifted education and general education: Toward communication, cooperation, and collaboration. *Gifted Child Quarterly, 40,* 165–171.

VanTassel-Baska, J. (1992). Educational decision making on acceleration and grouping. *Gifted Child Quarterly, 36,* 68–72.

Ward, S. B., & Landrum, M. S. (1994). Resource consultation: An alternative service delivery model for gifted education. *Roeper Review, 16,* 275–279.

Westberg, K. L., Dobyns, S., & Archambault, F. X. (1993). *Observation manual for the Classroom Practices Record (CPR).* Storrs, CT: National Research Center for the Gifted and Talented, The University of Connecticut.

8

Evaluation of a Full-Time Self-Contained Class for Gifted Students

Joyce VanTassel-Baska

College of William and Mary

Gordon B. Willis

Northwestern University

Donna Meyer

South Bend (IN) Community Schools

Controlled studies of the effectiveness of gifted programs are rare. An evaluative study of the Depth gifted program in South Bend, Indiana, was carried out using a control group, pre-post measurement, and multiple outcome measures. It was found that on a general test of cognitive ability, program participants exhibited significantly higher gains than did controls, and participants rated the quality of their school life more highly at the end of the program. The study lends support to the benefits of self-contained gifted programs.

Editor's Note: From VanTassel-Baska, J., Willis, G. B., Meyer, D. (1989). Evaluation of a full-time self-contained class for gifted students. *Gifted Child Quarterly, 33*(1), 7-10. © 1989 National Association for Gifted Children. Reprinted with permission.

Very little research has focused on the effects of student participation in gifted programs. In a review of the research literature, Gallagher, Weiss, Oglesby, and Thomas (1983) cited fewer than forty such studies, and most of them involved no control or comparison group. Generally, a simple pre-post model was employed to demonstrate growth. In a more recent study, Traxler (1987) found that while evaluations of gifted programs were now more frequently carried out, only 50% were designed before program implementation and slightly less than 30% involved trained evaluators. Feldhusen and Treffinger (1985) reviewed all the research on full-time, self-contained classes for the gifted and concluded that such classes are needed truly to meet the needs of gifted students.

Part of the problem rests with the evaluation methodology available to demonstrate effectiveness in gifted programs. Tests must be carefully selected and piloted for potential ceiling effects. Another part of the problem is understanding how evaluation results can be utilized to improve programs for the gifted. Too frequently evaluation reports are merely shelved. Callahan and Caldwell (1984) synthesized the literature on effective utilization of evaluation results and found that the conceptualization of the evaluation process, the credibility of information, the timing, and the feasibility of the evaluation are the most critical elements determining usefulness. Carter and Hamilton (1985) noted the problem of relying on attitudinal data rather than data on student growth or change to validate program effectiveness.

Approaches that should be used in evaluating gifted programs have also been delineated in the literature. Archambault (1984) advocated the use of better quantitative designs in gifted education to measure program outcomes as well as qualitative procedures. Some researchers have viewed naturalistic evaluation as useful in special program areas like gifted education as long as systematic procedures are followed and triangulation of results is obtained from multiple data sources (Stake, 1975; Barnette, 1984). Kulieke (1986) presented a model for evaluation that rated various designs according to the major purposes of the program so that a good match of program approach and evaluation methodology might be effected.

METHOD

Subjects. This study used a self-contained gifted class of 3rd and 4th graders (Depth) from the South Bend Community School Corporation, South Bend, Indiana. All students were selected for the program from one high school attendance district in the city by a combination of identification measures that included general ability inventories, achievement data, and recommendations from educational personnel. All children in the program exhibited advanced development in terms of functional school ability as evidenced by being at or above the 95th percentile on the selection measure: the total battery of the Iowa Test of Basic Skills, The Cognitive Abilities Test, and a checklist of behavioral characteristics associated with academic talent. A control group of students also exhibiting these score levels on the instruments cited was selected from another school district in the city.

Putting the Research to Use

This study presents some key ideas for practitioners seeking to demonstrate student growth in full-time self-contained classes for the gifted. Several features of the study that might be considered for replication in other districts include: 1) the use of a control or comparison group outside of the school district; 2) the use of multiple measures to ascertain perceptions of student growth; 3) the use of a combination of measures—standard tests, inventories, and questionnaires; and 4) the use of goal-based evaluation, in which a district attempts to find out how well students are progressing toward the goals of the program. Additionally the study lends credence to the case for self-contained programs for the gifted as a mechanism for enhancing the potential of gifted learners.

The Program Treatment. The experimental group of gifted students participated in a special program (Depth) on a full-time basis in one building of the city. The Depth program had four major objectives:

- Improve critical thinking and inquiry;
- Enhance self-concept;
- Promote a positive attitude toward school and the learning process;
- Provide opportunities for the interaction of intellectually gifted students.

These objectives were addressed through a curriculum that was rich in individual and small group activities, that employed critical thinking activities as an overlay to basic content, and that provided a context for student discussion and idea generation. Teachers in the program used outside speakers and the community to help in the learning process. Key features of the program, as delineated by the gifted program coordinator, included: a focus on higher level thinking, opportunities for divergent production, exposure to core content based on readiness, and teacher effectiveness. The Depth program differs from the regular program by placing more emphasis on the following curriculum considerations:

1. The compression or deletion of material that is mastered quickly or has been mastered on the student's own.

2. Concentration on higher level thinking skills.

3. Concentration on the interrelationships among bodies of knowledge.

4. Use of content areas that offer appropriate challenge—logic, philosophy, foreign language.

5. Inclusion of a guidance component that focuses on coping with talent.

6. Independent study assignments.

7. Self-directed learning.

Additionally, the teachers in the program have developed a scope and sequence of key skills and concepts to be taught for language arts, mathematics, science, and social studies. The control group received no special program or curriculum and was assigned to different teachers at the same grade levels.

Procedure

The intent of this evaluation was to ascertain cognitive and affective outcomes of the Depth program in the South Bend Community Schools at the end of one year. The evaluation instruments were varied in nature, ranging from tests of cognitive ability to subjective self-reports by students and parents. In this way, multiple outcomes could potentially be measured in a manner that would provide important data for future program changes and improvements.

Subjects were given the *Ross Test of Cognitive Abilities* at the beginning and at the end of the academic year to determine gains in key critical thinking areas. A second measure administered to both groups was the *Quality of School Life Scale (QSL)*, a questionnaire that determines the degree of positive reaction to a student's school situation. A third instrument used was the *ME* (Feldhusen & Kolloff, 1981) scale, an instrument that measures self-concept among gifted children. Validity and reliability data were available for all instruments and judged to be satisfactory for research purposes. A parent questionnaire was also used to measure attitudes toward and perceived benefits of the program.

RESULTS

Statistical tests of differences between or among means were judged significant if they reached the .05 level. Analysis of covariance (ANCOVA) on the pre-post results of the *Ross Test* suggested that there was a positive effect of the Depth program; on the posttest, mean scores were significantly higher ($p < .05$) for the Depth group than for the control group. The average overall Ross pretest scores for the groups of 19 experimental and 20 control subjects were 54.8 and 54.5, respectively. The difference between these groups is not statistically significant. Scores on the three subscales comprising the *Ross Test* (Analytic, Synthetic, and Evaluative) also did not differ between groups. On the posttest, the mean total scores were 70.9 for the Depth group and 64.7 for the control. This difference

Table 1   Mean Scores of Depth and Control Group Students on the Ross Test of Cognitive Abilities: Overall Score and Subscale Scores

| | DEPTH (Experimental) | | | CONTROL | | |
	Pre	Post	Difference	Pre	Post	Difference
Overall	54.8 (8.7)[1]	70.9 (10.3)	16.1*	54.5 (10.9)	64.7 (9.5)	10.2
Analytic	16.2 (4.3)	22.4 (4.2)	6.2*	16.7 (4.0)	19.1 (5.0)	2.4
Synthetic	19.2 (4.6)	26.5 (4.8)	7.3	18.4 (5.5)	24.3 (3.2)	5.9
Evaluative	19.5 (3.3)	22.0 (4.3)	2.5	19.5 (3.3)	21.4 (3.7)	1.9

*Significant at the .05 level.

[1]Numbers in parentheses are standard deviations.

was not significant. Analysis of the subscales showed a significant superiority of the Depth group on the posttest for the Analytic scale but no significant differences on the Synthetic scale or the Evaluative scale (See Table 1).

The average gain on the overall Ross score for the Depth group was 16.1 points, and for the control group, 10.2 points. This difference is significant. It was concluded that the Depth program produced a greater overall increase than did the control. There was also a significantly greater increase for the Depth group than for the control group on the analysis subscale.

In analysing the Quality of Life scale, mean scores on the overall test and on its subscales (Satisfaction, Commitment to Classwork, and Reaction to Teachers) were found to be greater for the Depth than for the control group (See Table 2). These differences were statistically significant for the Total score, the Commitment score, and Reaction to Teachers. Using fifth grade norms, analysis reveals that the Depth group may be generally classed as "high" in overall rating in Reaction to Teacher and in Satisfaction, and medium-high in Commitment to School-Work. The control group is within the "medium" category in all areas of the instrument. In short, the Depth group may be characterized as positive in its evaluation of the school experience, while the control group is more neutral.

On the *ME* scale of self-concept, the average score out of 36 was 28.8 for the Depth group and 30.9 for the control group. This difference was not statistically significant. Two observations may be made. First, the average scores are high based on mean score comparisons; both groups exhibit a high self-concept at posttest administration. Second, it may be an important finding that the experimental group was not found to be low in self-concept. One of the potential outcomes of special classes can be that some gifted students with previous histories of academic superiority feel inferior to classmates and thus experience a decrease in self-concept. The data suggest that the Depth program did not cause a lowering of self-concept, although absolute differences cannot be assessed due to lack of pretesting on this dimension.

The return rate of the parent questionnaires was relatively high; 78% for the Depth group and 75% for the control group. Although the questionnaires are

Table 2   Mean Scores of Depth and Control Group Students on the Quality of School Life Scale (QSL): Overall Score and Subscale Scores

	DEPTH (Experimental)		CONTROL		EFFECT SIZE
Overall	21.7	(4.4)	16.7*	(7.7)	.79
Reaction to Teacher	8.9	(2.1)	6.6*	(3.5)	.79
Commitment to Schoolwork	8.8	(2.2)	6.9	(3.0)	.72
Satisfaction	4.1	(1.4)	3.3	(1.7)	.51

*Difference between groups significant at the .05 level.
Note: Numbers in parentheses are standard deviation values.

not strictly comparable because different questions were asked of the two groups, six questions were identical across questionnaires and were therefore analyzed. The mean ratings given by parents to these questions are given in Table 3. Ratings are on a scale of either 1–4 or 1–5, with the high value indicating strong agreement, and a 1 representing equally strong disagreement. On all evaluative questions, ratings for the Depth group were significantly higher than for the control group. The mean response to the question asking for an overall rating of the program was 4.7 out of 5 for the Depth group, indicating that parents were extremely pleased with the program quality. Interestingly, the one question that produced overwhelmingly strong agreement in both groups was one concerning the desirability of grouping like-ability students.

Representative comments provided by parents of children in the Depth group verify what was suggested by the ratings:

1. The class creates a mutual competitiveness without the fear of failure or (more importantly) the embarrassment of being "too smart."

2. She has renewed interest in school and her ability to learn. She has developed a true feeling of belonging and closeness with the other students in the class.

3. He has learned more responsibility. He has been academically challenged for the first time. Also his attitude toward school has improved. He hated it before.

DISCUSSION

The separate parts of the analysis combine to express a consistent theme; over the course of one academic year, the Depth program produced a wide range of positive outcomes in comparison to a normal classroom environment. Students and parents appear to have been strongly supportive of both the need for this general type of program and for the particular program that was implemented.

Table 3   Mean Scores of Depth and Control Group Students on the Evaluation
Questionnaire

	DEPTH (Experimental)		CONTROL		EFFECT SIZE
1. Overall rating of quality of child's schooling	4.7	(0.6)	3.9*	(1.0)	.98
2. Program meets educational needs of the child	4.4	(0.8)	3.5*	(1.2)	.05
3. Important to have grouping of students with similar ability	4.7	(0.6)	4.5	(0.9)	.26
4. Students have positive attitude toward school	3.6	(0.6)	3.0*	(0.9)	.79
5. Student expresses enjoyment about work done in school	3.7	(0.5)	3.3*	(0.6)	.73
6. Child finds work done in school to be challenging	3.5	(0.5)	3.0*	(0.6)	.91

*Difference between groups significant at the .05 level.

Note: Questions 1, 2, and 3 are on 5 item scale, with 5 = strong agreement and 1 = strong
disagreement.
Questions 4, 5, and 6 are on a 4 item scale, with 4 = often and 1 = never.
Numbers in parentheses are standard deviation values.

Student participants suffered no damage to self-concept as a result of the
program, and they ranked their quality of school life as very high. Cognitive
test scores further support the value of the Depth program; the Depth children
were found to outperform control children significantly at the end of treatment.

The current study provides some valuable information on effective
approaches to evaluation of gifted programs. The multiple outcome measures
allowed for a mixture of quantitative and qualitative assessment. The control
group made true comparison of results possible. The attempt to measure the
stated objectives of a gifted program was also successful. Even though some
objectives were in the affective area, the instruments assessed some of the most
important constructs: attitude toward school and self-concept.

The study also contributes to the small body of literature that documents
the positive impact of full-time, self-contained classes on gifted students.
Follow-up studies on the Depth program should be done to assess further
growth of students in the area of thinking skills and other aspects of the
curriculum.

REFERENCES

Archambault, F. X. (1984). Measurement and evaluation concerns in evaluating programs for the gifted and talented. *Journal for the Education of the Gifted, 7,* 12–25.

Barnette, J. J. (1984). Naturalistic approaches to gifted and talented program evaluation. *Journal for the Education of the Gifted, 7,* 26–37.

Callahan, C., & Caldwell, M. (1984). Using evaluation results to improve programs for the gifted and talented. *Journal for the Education of the Gifted, 7,* 60–74.

Carter, K. R., & Hamilton, W. (1985). Formative evaluation of gifted programs: A process and model. *Gifted Child Quarterly, 29,* 5–11.

Feldhusen, J. F., & Kolloff, M. B. (1981). ME: A self-concept scale for gifted students. *Perceptual and Motor Skills, 53,* 319–323.

Feldhusen, J. F., & Treffinger, D. J. (1985). *Creative thinking and problem solving in gifted education.* Dubuque, IA: Kendall/Hunt.

Gallagher, J. J. (1981). *A report on the national survey.* Paper presented at the National Association for Gifted Children, Portland, OR.

Gallagher, J. J., Weiss, P., Oglesby, K., & Thomas, T. (1983). *The status of gifted/talented education: United States survey of needs, practices and policies.* Los Angeles: Leadership Training Institute.

Kulieke, M. (1986). *An evaluation handbook on assessing the impact of programs for gifted learners,* Evanston, IL: Center for Talent Development, Northwestern University.

Stake, R. E. (1975). *Program evaluation.* Occasional paper series, No. 5, Kalamazoo, MI: Evaluation Center, Western Michigan University.

Traxler, M. A. (1987). Gifted education program evaluation: A national review. *Journal for the Education of the Gifted, 10,* 107–113.

9

Expert Benchmarks for Student Academic Performance: The Case for Gifted Children

Eva L. Baker

John Schacter

University of California, Los Angeles

A discussion of the use of expert performance as the basis for inferring assessment scoring criteria is presented. Characteristics of experts are discussed, leading to a consideration of the appropriateness of using adult experts' performance to measure children's performance. The use of a priori classifications of children is explored, and the suggestion for examining the use of gifted students' performances as benchmarks is presented. Both positive and negative consequences are described.

Editor's Note: From Baker, E. L., & Schacter, J. (1996). In the public interest. Expert benchmarks for student academic performance: The case for gifted children. *Gifted Child Quarterly, 40*(2), 61-65. © 1996 National Association for Gifted Children. Reprinted with permission.

Current models for assessing complex student performance involve training raters to score performance against a set of standards and criteria developed by experts in the content domain. Years of research at the Center for Research on Evaluation, Standards, and Student Testing (CRESST) have evidenced that raters can be trained to reliably score complex performance, and that this methodology for measuring student performance is valid (Abedi, Baker & Herl, 1993; Baker 1994b; Baker, Aschbacher, et al. 1991; Baker Freeman, & Clayton, 1991; Herl, 1995; Herl, Niemi, & Baker, 1995; Shavelson, Lang, & Lewin, 1994). A fundamental issue is: What standards are used and how are valid criteria developed for scoring. The choice and specificity of any scoring approach will also vary to some degree as the purpose for the assessment varies. That is, assessments designed to report for general accountability may have less complete or detailed criteria than those intended to assist teachers in providing additional supportive instruction for students not yet reaching performance goals. However, as new policies emerge pushing the multiple use of single assessment options, it is very likely that, in the future, much of educational assessment will attempt to provide results useful for both accountability and instructional improvement.

To date two major strategies have been used in the development of scoring criteria. The first depends entirely on the discussion, analysis, and agreement of teachers and other curriculum experts on the sorts of performance that ought to be expected of students and on the key elements in scoring. This approach, briefly described in Baker (1994b) focuses on the discussion of what "should" be in student responses and how to score them against these criteria. The second approach involves looking at what "experts" do rather than what teachers say. Some research has contrasted expert and novice performance (Baker, 1994a; Baker, Freeman, & Clayton, 1991; O'Neil, Allred, & Dennis, in press; O'Neil, Baker, Ni, Jacoby, & Swigger, 1994; O'Neil, Chung, & Brown, in press). The benefit of this approach is that it is concrete—grounded in actual performance rather than in general desires—and thus brings with it a strong aura of validity. That is, if students' performance maps to what an expert in a particular field does, then it seems more reasonable to trust the criteria evolved from such expert performance.

Over the past six years CRESST has employed expert knowledge models to assess student performance in a number of content domains. CRESST's scoring methods have used components from both of the expert model research studies described above. On problem-solving tasks, a science performance assessment constructed by Baxter, Elder, and Glaser (1995) for CRESST rated student problem-solving performance according to four dimensions. Proficient students were characterized by their ability to (a) integrate knowledge that fosters their ability to reason, explain, and make inferences with what they know; (b) effectively represent the meaning of a problem and plan an approach before employing a solution strategy; (c) select a strategy for problem solving that is reasoned and efficient, not a trial-and-error process; and (d) employ a repertoire of well-developed self-regulatory skills to monitor their performance. These scoring criteria were extrapolated from studies of experts. Students were rated on a four-point scale for each of these abilities. Comprehensive criteria for rating students' complex performance showed that high- and low-scoring students displayed qualitatively different performance characteristics. High-scoring students demonstrated in their explanations a generalized understanding of the principles underlying the content domain; they displayed a systematic approach to solving the problem by gathering all possible information before drawing conclusions; and they engaged in effective and flexible monitoring of their performance by referring to their prior investigations and operating within the constraints of the task (Baker, Aschbacher, Niemi, & Sato, 1992; Baxter et al., 1995).

Putting the Research to Use

Setting performance criteria presents educators with the choice among several options. It might be possible to use adult expert performance as the benchmark for assessment. A second possibility would be to use the performances of teachers with content expertise to establish the criteria of excellent performance as they have both content and pedagogical knowledge. A third possibility might be to use more developmentally appropriate models, the performances of identified gifted students, for example. Using high-performing student examples to set scoring criteria has the advantage of using work done by children rather than adults as the model. Finally, in order to set higher yet reasonable standards, educators might use student performances one or two grade levels ahead of those being assessed. The first two adult models have generated a research base. The two child models have yet to be investigated. Educators working with gifted children and youth have the opportunity to further both research and practice by systematically collecting work samples and performances of child models of assessment.

EXPERT PERFORMANCE

Studies of expert performance have been used in research to uncover the structure of knowledge in particular fields. Some have studied the contrast between experts and novices while learning. By examining a set of experts' processes and performances and comparing that behavior with novices' performance, these researchers highlight differences in how experts both structure and use their knowledge (Chi, 1978; Gentner 1988; Johnson, 1988; Larkin, 1983; Lawrence, 1988;

Lesgold et al., 1988; Miyake & Norman, 1979; Simon & Simon, 1978; Voss & Post, 1988). Others have focused on expert performance to design and evaluate complex systems (Kieras, 1988; Means & Gott, 1988; O'Neil et al., 1994; Shank & Kass, 1988; Staggers & Norcio, 1993). Overall expert performance tends to be principled, highly automatized, and dependent on organized prior knowledge. These general standards may make real experts too remote from the performance of learners as they engage initially in a particular discipline. What other options are there?

ARE TEACHERS THE BEST APPROXIMATION OF STUDENT EXPERTISE?

Teachers may be viewed as potentially valid expert models because they have subject matter expertise as well as pedagogical expertise. To our knowledge, two studies have used teacher expertise as the performance against which student efforts were compared. These studies used teachers' knowledge representations in a concept mapping task as a basis to assess students' knowledge representations in the same topic areas (Herl, 1995; Lomask, Baron, Greig, & Harrison, 1992). Herl (1995) used teachers who had reliably scored students' essays about the Great Depression to construct closed concept maps, that is, maps with predetermined link terms (possible relationships) and a predetermined set of nodes (declarative knowledge). Selecting teachers who had been trained to score student essays was adopted as a strategy because it was expected that these teachers would have a deeper understanding of topic knowledge. Herl (1995) compared 11th-grade students' concept maps to four expert teacher maps. The semantic content scores of the concept maps were based on the semantic links constructed by experts in their maps. Each expert's map was then used to compute a total map score for each student, resulting in four computer-generated scores for each student map. This deep pattern matching analysis of concepts and relationships used by students compared to terms and links used by expert teachers approximated how closely student maps resembled expert teacher maps.

Herl's (1995) approach is interesting because it is based simultaneously on teachers' own content expertise and on their perception of student performance. Because teachers were exposed to student essays prior to developing maps, there is the presumption that teacher maps were more congruent with what content was included in student essays. However, this hypothesis is unexplored.

HOW MANY EXPERTS?

Variation among experts as sources of knowledge is also an issue. In Herl's study, four experts were used, and a compilation of their maps served as the expert template for scoring student performance. The number of experts to choose for comparative assessment purposes is further complicated by developmental factors. One predominant factor is that adult knowledge representations will vary more than children's. Because adults' knowledge is more developed, their representations will be more detailed and elaborate than third-grade students' representations. Elaborate knowledge representations may exhibit higher degrees of variability within content domains, creating additional technical problems for inferring key criteria for scoring purposes. Obviously, situations where criteria vary widely have different educational assessment utilities. In certain cases, variability may signal a general lack of agreement in the field and therefore designing scoring criteria that seek conformance would be inappropriate. Other areas, for instance, where the goal being measured is the innovation used in problem solving, would by their very nature depend upon differences in approach and detail. Scoring student responses would require extrapolation from the expert's or teacher's performance to key attributes of success, for instance, parsimony, unpredictable associations, and so on. Stevens (Stevens & Lopo, 1994; Stevens, Wang, & Lopo, in press) used hundreds of experts in the development of his computer-aided scoring system, particularly because he uses an approach that depends upon making a set of reasoned inferences from expert performance. His work demonstrates that multiple paths may be taken by experts, but in particular scientific areas, agreement on "correct" answers is possible.

Using expert-based scoring is not without its practical difficulties, however. It is fine to use experts' performance when there is a realistic goal that the student will approach such a level of performance. For example, it seems reasonable to hold a surgical resident up to the standard of an expert in evaluating her competence to perform life-saving procedures. It may also be appropriate to ask high school students to use the elements incorporated in expert performance in their essay responses to a history question. We understand that experts in responding to essay-type questions about major historical events invariably take points of views, focus on principles or major themes, and invoke relevant prior knowledge. Our expectation is not that given students will directly exemplify full expertise (difficult for even the most wondrous of high school students) but rather that they will begin to approximate expertise by including the key elements found in expert responses. For example, prior knowledge should be a fundamental component of an essay response, but the prior knowledge selected by students when compared with that provided by experts will likely be less pertinent, less elaborated, and less deftly connected to the organizing themes or principles.

When confronting the problem of expert-based criteria for younger students, however, we are left to struggle with the feasibility issue. Is it reasonable to expect a young student, say a fourth grader, to approach in any way the performance of a serious expert? For instance, can we expect third-grade students to formulate specific facts into general principles? If they do not succeed, are the inferences drawn from their performance more appropriate to an instructional or to a developmental hypothesis? How can we use the models of experts to generate scoring criteria if our usual sources, adult experts, are developmentally inappropriate?

If we are to attempt to validate an approach that takes into account developmentally appropriate expert performance, we are seemingly left with one that is based upon examples of performance by successful students. We should want to find the best performance we can obtain from experts who share important characteristics with our target learners. Adult experts are so defined because of jobs they hold, degrees they possess or other external variables. Our problem is to find an analogous basis of classification for student experts so that the work of such individuals can be inspected to determine its utility for the generation of assessment criteria. Essentially what we are looking for is a classification system that would allow us to distinguish student work in a manner similar to expert-novice comparisons.

WHAT ABOUT HIGH-PERFORMING STUDENTS AS A SOURCE OF PERFORMANCE BENCHMARKS?

We are suggesting for consideration the use of performance from high-performing students. We could approximate expert performance in American history for a fifth-grade student by looking systematically at the performance of gifted fifth-grade students. Their work would be collected, used as models for what is desirable, and inspected in order to infer common features that could be explicated as scorable criteria for assessments. This strategy is not unlike approaches that ask judges simply to sort performance into high and low categories and then infer distinctions (Baker, Freeman, & Clayton, 1991). There are important differences however. First, an a priori classification base for students exists. One common way students are classified by external criteria includes grades; yet, grading practices vary considerably and are subject to highly local standards. More common practices may exist for the identification of gifted and talented children, although there is still some debate about the contribution of intelligence to the variance. As Sternberg and Clinkenbeard (1995) state, "Scholars may disagree as to what abilities should be considered to identify giftedness, but most will agree that current procedures sample only a narrow band of the broad range of human abilities" (p. 255). Based upon whatever practice was used, it would be possible to explore the utility of this approach in terms of the validity of the findings produced when using scoring criteria inferred from such students. It would also be desirable to determine what other attributes were included in gifted students' performance that were irregularly found in the performance of competent children not so classified. The performance of gifted students would be used as a source of benchmarks and then studied in order to infer scoring criteria.

Gifted students possess many of the cognitive qualities of expert performers. Gifted children on average exhibit high levels of metacognitive abilities (Cheng, 1993; Rogers, 1986). They monitor their thinking, select appropriate strategies, allocate attentional resources and evaluate their solution processes in an iterative way. High-performing children and especially gifted children seem more adept at figuring out what is required of them with less information supplied (Sternberg, 1988). To do this, gifted students spend a nontrivial amount of time performing global planning strategies that help them constrain and solve complex problems (Sternberg, 1981). Like experts, gifted students have large domain-dependent knowledge structures which enable them to automate several tasks, and complete problems with high levels of speed and precision. This automaticity frees memory capacity for processing more difficult aspects of the task. Thus, gifted students demonstrate high performance in both short-term and long-term recall because they have automatized tasks that would have otherwise demanded their attention (Chi, Glaser, & Farr, 1988; Sternberg, 1977).

Expert performers' strength is in coding and identifying relevant variables (Johnson, 1988). Gifted students also have the skill for sifting out relevant from irrelevant information. Gifted students are also quite adept at combining what might seem like isolated pieces of information into a unified whole. This ability involves relating what is known to what is being learned. Similar to expert performers, gifted students represent problems by constructing and running mental models (Sternberg, 1988). Building mental representations of the problem helps problem solvers infer relations that can define the situation and increase understanding of how the system works (Gentner & Gentner, 1983; Glaser & Chi, 1988; Mayer, 1989). Thus, gifted students share many cognitive similarities with experts. Like experts, they capitalize on patterns of information, have exceptional metacognitive and problem finding skills, conceive higher order relations, have automated much of their knowledge, and form mental representations of the problems they are solving (Sternberg & Davidson, 1986). All of these reasons support using gifted students as developmentally appropriate expert performance benchmarks, but there may be reservations as well.

APPROPRIATENESS OF GIFTED PERFORMANCE MODELS

One strong concern regarding this proposal is that it may set unreasonable standards for students to achieve, essentially substituting one inappropriate set of experts (adult experts) with another (gifted students). Sternberg and Clinkenbeard (1995) argue that analytic skills, creative synthetic skills, and practical contextual skills are three distinct sets of human abilities important within the school environment as well as outside of it.

Other researchers contend that the components of giftedness can be fostered and created. According to Ericsson, Krampe, and Tesch-Romer (1993), years of sustained deliberate practice within one domain (i.e., three to four hours each day) combined with masterful teachers and coaches within that domain can produce exceptional performers regardless of the individual's intellect. In a review of exceptional performance, Ericsson, Krampe, and Heizmann (1993) illustrated that innate capacities and abilities appear to play a minor, even "possibly a negligible role in the attainment of expert performance among normal children and adults" (p. 230). Ericsson's findings point to the importance of motivation, self-directedness, and highly disciplined behavior, which lead to individuals who achieve greatness. These attributes are those to be fostered by schools as well, although the capacity for developing such characteristics under present circumstances is extraordinarily limited.

Furthermore, there may very well be public consequences of using the performance of identified gifted students as the target of performance for most children. There may be a greater sense that such standards are unreachable and the province of unusual people rather than something to which more children and their teachers should aspire. Alternatives to "identified gifted" as classification of students can be imagined. One choice is to look at the performance of students one or two grades ahead of the grade being assessed. This approach may be acceptable at certain grade ranges and greatly inappropriate for those ages where developmental differences accelerate. A series of experimental strategies should be explored to determine what are reasonable, justified, non-arbitrary scoring criteria that will lead to valid inferences about individual student performance, school effectiveness, and educational accountability. For too long, the educational community has been criticized for setting its sights too low. Raising them is not without risk.

REFERENCES

Abedi, J., Baker, E. L., & Herl, H. (1993). *Comparing reliabilities obtained by different approaches for performance assessment.* Paper presented at the annual meeting of the American Educational Research Association, Atlanta.

Baker, E. L. (1994a). Human benchmarking of natural language systems. In H. F. O'Neil & E. L. Baker (Ed.) *Technology assessment in software applications* (pp. 85–97). Hillsdale, NJ: Lawrence Erlbaum Associates.

Baker, E. L. (1994b). Learning-based assessments of history understanding. *Educational Psychologist, 29*(2), 97–106.

Baker, E. L., Aschbacher, P., Niemi, D., & Sato, E. (1992). *CRESST performance assessment models: Assessing content area explanations.* Los Angeles: University of California, National Center for Research on Evaluation, Standards, and Student Testing.

Baker, E. L., Aschbacher, P., Niemi, D., Chang, S., Weinstock, M. & Herl, H. (1991). *Validating measures of deep understanding of history.* Paper presented at the annual meeting of the American Educational Research Association, Chicago.

Baker, E. L., Freeman, M., & Clayton, S. (1991). Cognitive assessment of history for large-scale testing. In M. C. Wittrock & E. L. Baker (Eds.), *Testing and cognition* (pp. 131–153). Englewood, NJ: Prentice Hall.

Baxter, G. P., Elder, A. D., Glaser, R. (1995). *Cognitive analysis of a science performance assessment* (CSE Technical Report 398). Los Angeles: University of California, Center for Research on Evaluation, Standards, and Student Testing.

Cheng, P. W. (1993). Metacognition and giftedness: The state of the relationship. *Gifted Child Quarterly, 37*, 105–112.

Chi, M. T. H. (1978). Knowledge structures and memory development. In R. Siegler (Ed.), *Children's thinking: What develops?* (pp. 73–96). Hillsdale, NJ: Lawrence Erlbaum Associates.

Chi, M. T., Glaser; R., & Farr, M. J. (1988). *The nature of expertise.* Hillsdale, NJ: Lawrence Erlbaum Associates.

Ericsson, K. A., Krampe, R. T., & Heizmann, S. (1993). Can we create gifted people? In Ciba Foundation, *The origins and development of high ability* (pp. 222–249). New York: John Wiley & Sons.

Ericsson, K. A., Krampe, R. T., & Tesch-Romer, C. (1993). The role of deliberate practice in the acquisition of expert performance. *Psychology Review, 100,* 363–406.

Gentner D., & Gentner, D. R. (1983). Flowing waters or teeming crowds: Mental models of electricity. In D. Gentner & A. L. Stevens (Eds.), *Mental models* (pp. 99–129). Hillsdale, NJ: Lawrence Erlbaum Associates.

Gentner, D. R. (1988). Expertise in typewriting. In M. T. H. Chi, R. Glaser, & M. J. Farr (Ed.), *The nature of expertise* (pp. 1–22). Hillsdale, NJ: Lawrence Erlbaum Associates.

Glaser, R., & Chi, M. T. H. (1988). Overview. In M. T. H. Chi, R. Glaser, & M. J. Farr (Eds.), *The nature of expertise* (pp. xv–xxviii). Hillsdale, NJ: Lawrence Erlbaum Associates.

Herl, H. E. (1995). *Construct validation of an approach to modeling cognitive structure of experts' and novices' U.S. history knowledge.* Unpublished doctoral dissertation, University of California, Los Angeles.

Herl, H., Niemi, D., & Baker, E. I., (1995). *Construct validation of an approach to modeling cognitive structure of experts' and novices' U.S. history knowledge.* Paper presented at the annual meeting of the American Educational Research Association, San Francisco.

Johnson, E. J. (1988). Expertise and decision under uncertainty: Performance and process. In M. T. H. Chi, R. Glaser; & M. J. Farr (Eds.), *The nature of expertise* (pp. 209–228). Hillsdale, NJ: Lawrence Erlbaum Associates.

Kieras, D. E. (1988). What mental model should be taught: Choosing instructional content for complex engineered systems. In J. Psotka, L. D. Massey, & S. A. Mutter (Eds.), *Intelligent tutoring systems: Lessons learned* (pp. 85–111). Hillsdale, NJ: Lawrence Erlbaum Associates.

Larkin, J. H. (1983). The role of problem representation in physics. In D. Gentner & A. L. Stevens (Eds.), *Mental models* (pp. 75–100). Hillsdale, NJ: Lawrence Erlbaum Associates.

Lawrence, J. A. (1988). Expertise on the bench: Modeling magistrates' judicial decision-making. In M. T. H. Chi, R. Glaser, & M. J. Farr (Eds.), *The nature of expertise* (pp. 229–260). Hillsdale, NJ: Lawrence Erlbaum Associates.

Lesgold, A., Rubinson, H., Feltovich, P., Glaser, R. Klopfer D., & Wang, Y. (1988). Expertise in a complex skill: Diagnosing X-ray pictures. In M. T. H. Chi, R. Glaser, & M. J. Farr (Eds.), *The nature of expertise* (pp. 311–342). Hillsdale, NJ: Lawrence Erlbaum Associates.

Lomask, M., Baron, J., Greig, J., & Harrison, C. (1992). *ConnMap: Connecticut's use of concept mapping to assess the structure of students' knowledge of science.* Symposium presented at the annual meeting of the National Center for Research in Science Teaching and Learning, Cambridge, MA.

Mayer, R. E. (1989). Models for understanding. *Review of Educational Research, 59*(1), 43–64.

Means, B., & Gott, S. P. (1988). Cognitive task analysis as a basis for tutor development: Articulating abstract knowledge representations. In J. Psotka, L. D. Massey, & S. A. Mutter

(Eds.), *Intelligent tutoring systems: Lessons learned* (pp. 35–57). Hillsdale, NJ: Lawrence Erlbaum Associates.

Miyake, N., & Norman, D. A. (1979). To ask a question one must know enough to know what is not known. *Journal of Verbal Learning and Verbal Behavior, 18*, 357–364.

O'Neil, H. F., Jr., Allred, K., & Dennis, R. A. (in press). Assessment issues in the validation of a computer simulation of negotiation skills. In H. F. O'Neil, Jr., (Ed.), *Workforce readiness: Competencies and assessment*. Mahwah, NJ: Lawrence Erlbaum Associates.

O'Neil, H. E. Jr., Baker, E. L., Ni, Y., Jacoby, A., & Swigger, K. M. (1994). Human benchmarking for the evaluation of expert systems. In H. F. O'Neil, Jr., & E. L. Baker (Eds.) *Technology assessment in software applications* (pp. 13–45). Hillsdale, NJ: Lawrence Erlbaum Associates.

O'Neil, H. E. Jr., Chung, G., & Brown, R. (in press). Use of networked simulations as a context to measure team competencies. In H. F. O'Neil, Jr., (Ed.), *Workforce readiness: Competencies and assessment*. Mahwah, NJ: Lawrence Erlbaum Associates.

Rogers, K. (1986). Do the gifted think and learn differently? A review of recent research and its implications for instruction. *Journal for the Education of the Gifted, 10*, 17–39.

Shank, R., & Kass, A. (1988). Knowledge representation in people and machines. In U. Eco, M. Santambrogio, & P. Violi (Eds.), *Meaning and mental representations* (pp. 181–200). Bloomington: Indiana University Press.

Shavelson, R. J., Lang, H., & Lewin, B. (1994). *On concept maps as potential "authentic" assessments in science* (CSE Tech. Rep. No. 388). Los Angeles: University of California, National Center for Research on Evaluation, Standards, and Student Testing.

Simon, D. P. & Simon, H. A. (1978). Individual differences in solving physics problems. In R. Siegler (Ed.), *Children's thinking: What develops?* (pp. 325–348). Hillsdale, NJ: Lawrence Erlbaum Associates.

Staggers, N., & Norcio, A. F. (1993). Mental models: Concepts for human-computer interaction research. *International Journal Man-Machine Studies, 38*, 587–605.

Sternberg, R. J. (1977). *Intelligence, information processing, and analogical reasoning: The componential analysis of human abilities.* Hillsdale, NJ: Lawrence Erlbaum Associates.

Sternberg, R. J. (1981). Intelligence and nonentrenchment. *Journal of Educational Psychology, 73*, 1–16.

Sternberg, R. J. (1988). A unified theory of intellectual exceptionality. In J. D. Day & J. G. Borkowski (Eds.), *Intelligence and exceptionality: New directions for theory, assessment, and instructional practices* (pp. 135–172). Norwood, NJ: Ablex

Sternberg, R. J., & Clinkenbeard, P. R. (1995). The triarchic model applied to identifying, teaching and assessing gifted children. *Roeper Review 17*(4), 255–260.

Sternberg, R. J., & Davidson, J. E. (1986). *Conceptions of giftedness.* New York: Cambridge University Press.

Stevens, R., & Lopo, A. (1994). Artificial neural network comparison of expert and novice problem-solving strategies. *Proceedings of the Eighteenth Annual Symposium on Computer Applications in Medical Care* (pp. 64–68).

Stevens, R., Wang, P., & Lopo, A. (in press). Artificial neural networks can distinguish novice and expert strategies during complex problem-solving. *Journal of the American Medical Informatics Association.*

Voss, J. E, & Post, T. A. (1988). On the solving of ill-structured problems. In M. T. H. Chi, R. Glaser, & M. J. Farr (Eds.), *The nature of expertise* (pp. 261–285). Hillsdale, NJ: Lawrence Erlbaum Associates.

10

Qualitative Assessment of Gifted Education

Sara W. Lundsteen

North Texas State University

This article describes qualitative research using an ethnographic perspective, with particular reference to gifted education. The purpose is to help the reader, through examples, to understand the potential use of qualitative assessment methods when studying and evaluating programs for gifted children. The sources include the published literature on qualitative research and studies on gifted education using an ethnographic perspective. The article concludes that more use of this methodology could be beneficial to the field of gifted education.

To rise from a zero
And be a great hero
To answer these questions you'll strive—
  "Where am I going
  How shall I get there, and
  How will I know I've arrived?"

(Mager, 1968)

Editor's Note: From Lundsteen, S. W. (1987). Qualitative assessment of gifted education. *Gifted Child Quarterly, 31*(1), 25-29. © 1987 National Association for Gifted Children. Reprinted with permission.

This portion of a longer verse was written by Mager in praise of the sort of "behavioral objective" with which most people in education are familiar. For illustration: "Given paper and pencil, a gifted student will be able to write a 200 word composition in 5 minutes with 98% spelling accuracy." Qualitative assessment does not typically use the specific data that Mager advocates. Nevertheless, it can be a highly productive way of answering questions about *where* the participants in gifted education *think* they are going, *how* they *think* they will get there, and *how* they *think* that they know they have arrived. Those questions take us to the purpose of this article, describing qualitative research or assessment, stressing an ethnographic perspective with reference to gifted education. First, the article treats the large umbrella of qualitative research; then the focal point of the ethnographic perspective.

CHARACTERISTICS OF QUALITATIVE RESEARCH

Five characteristics of *qualitative* research listed by Bogdan and Biklen (1982) are as follows:

1. *Qualitative research has the natural setting as the direct source of data, and the researcher is the key instrument.* Often the term *naturalistic* is used because the researcher observes and gathers data where the behavior under study is likely to occur; it happens naturally. To find out how gifted children use their time in a regular classroom, one may sit in a class in which some children identified as gifted are working.

2. *Qualitative research is descriptive.* The data tend to give us a "feel" for what people said, did, or indicated they were thinking about. It might include a written description of how some gifted children played with their peers during recess, or a videotape of how a gifted child constructed something artistic. Numerical data may also be used.

3. *Qualitative researchers are concerned with process as well as product.* For example, formative evaluators can check to see what children were chosen to join a gifted program, if the selection methods were actually followed, if the results were appropriate or inappropriate, and what the perceptions of the students were during the selection process.

4. *Qualitative researchers tend to analyze their data inductively.* What the researcher observes comes first, and out of that data are teased descriptive patterns, hypotheses, or even a theory. Going into the setting with ideas (hypotheses) has a role, but one must be flexible, amenable to change, as observations progress. One might go to a site with the idea that many gifted children waste their time in a regular classroom. On observation one might notice a child who finishes her work in a fraction of the typical time and then spends considerable time sitting at her desk "doing nothing." After repeated observations one

begins to feel time is being wasted. An interview is set up with that child; she explains that today she was working out in her mind how she could build a projectile which would travel further than the last one she made. This discovery might lead to more investigation of how gifted children really use their "spare" time.

5. *"Meaning" is of essential concern to the qualitative approach.* The perspective of the participants, the way they see their situation, environment, and behavior is of importance to the naturalistic researcher. How do different people make sense out of their lives? How do gifted children perceive their roles with each other, with their classmates, with their teacher, in their school? Since case studies (bounded systems—a child, a class) and other such forms of qualitative research are abundant, this article concentrates on an *ethnographic* perspective. Educational ethnographies are relatively new in the study of the gifted.

ETHNOGRAPHIC PERSPECTIVE

"Ethnographic *perspective*" is the studying and capturing of real-life processes of gifted education, ways of living in that social group context, its culture. *Culture* refers to people's on-going ways of perceiving, believing, evaluating, and acting (Goodenough, 1971). Within this perspective questions to ask are: "What's going on here? What are the behaviors and their meanings? What's stable, what's changing; what's predictable?" A question with a more limited focus might be, "Why are materials in this gifted program placed and used as they are?" Knowing the answers to such questions could be significant.

We can further ask: "What are the rules the children and teachers in this gifted classroom have to know, produce, predict, and evaluate in order to participate?" (Heath, 1982). Or, "How do the members of this gifted group hold each other accountable?" Such study will produce a description, one among many possible descriptions.

The ethnographic perspective (adapted to the educational setting) entails understanding the *participant's* perspective (e.g., the students' and the teachers' points of view). We get a picture of the people involved in their environment, such as classroom, school, home, community. We get a cultural history of group relations concerning gifted education. We see what social and cultural knowledge these participants bring to and generate in the setting. We can compare them transculturally with others. Such constructs are what is meant by ethnographic *perspective*.

ETHNOGRAPHIC PROCESS

Ethnographic perspective demands both a process and a product. A first-rate product requires a rigorous process. Some of these components are presented.

Theory

The method used with an ethnographic perspective is principled, even theoretically driven. But the use of the theory is highly flexible. The method creates the developmental growth of its own theories, grounding itself in past ethnographically-oriented work. Entering the setting open-minded is not going in empty-headed. We do have a body of explanatory ideas to relate to an ethnographic perspective for study of gifted children in their contexts. We need sets of explanations regarding what is occurring and what it means to others present. We need creative use of theory in this ethnographic method.

For example, in the Lutz and Lutz study (1981), reference is made to Terman's theoretical generalizations that gifted children are typically bigger than their less gifted peers. In the Lutz study, gifted children were not bigger. Some were even bullied by bigger ones who felt "bullied" by the superior intellect of the gifted students. They challenged Terman's generalization. In the Story (1985) study, theory was used to form a theoretical model of the roles played by the teacher of the gifted.

Use of Multiple Tools in Fieldwork

Besides using and developing theory, an ethnographic process demands use of multiple tools, not just one tool. In becoming functional human beings, we have all relied on numerous sources, taking ample time to attend to many (if not all) significant avenues. In qualitative research the use of several sources of data to discover and corroborate findings is referred to as *triangulation*. The method called triangulation contrasts with methods using few sources that are easy to count and understand. Some of the multiple tools used in ethnographic fieldwork are observation, interviews, written sources, and unwritten records.

Observation. A favored tool for the ethnographic perspective is *participant observation* with some form of permanent record (e.g., field notes, audio tape, camera shots, video tapes). Observation emphasizes examining the context in which behavior occurs while attempting to disturb the natural setting as little as possible. Nevertheless, there are degrees of participant observation ranging from limited (where the observer is very much an outsider) to highly involved (where the researcher interacts with the people under observation). A highly involved participant might be a teacher, observing the class he or she is teaching. Other participant observers might be students or researchers who participate in activities with the class.

Field notes. Field notes are an important part of observation with varying content. Five types of field notes may include:

1. *Frame setting information*—setting, arrangement of physical space, participant's behavior, verbatim language, gestures, time sequence, and the nature and duration of interaction episodes.

2. *Methodology*—records of methods used and plans of what the researcher may do next.

3. *Personal reactions*—enthnographer's personal feelings, human reactions, even frustrations (valuable for keeping these less scientific sources of bias separate).

4. *Inferences*—about gifted students, events, purposes, emotional tone, and processes.

5. *Theory*—pertaining to frameworks, models, patterns and constructs.

Each type of field note may be tied to an event, or a series of events, or "scenic units" (to borrow a term from TV script writing). Categories *emerge* from the record; categories are not predetermined. Then the researcher can look at specific meanings and contrasts across the scenic units in which individuals confront themselves or others.

Thus, a prime tool is observation and its field notes. But what does the ethnographer observe and when? The answer is "Well, it depends" (Wolcott, 1980). Observation is part of an inquiry process, with early observations serving to inform later ones and later ones influencing interpretation of earlier ones.

In the case of the present researcher, for example, it was not until we began to notice some style differences in behaviors from the video tapes of Swedish children engaged in creative problem-solving discussions that we decided to start asking ourselves questions about "style." We began by observing the children and administering tasks to help us gain an insight into the types of styles they were using. But as we got to know the American kindergarten teacher well, we could see the advisibility and feasibility of adding other tools to the research. For example, since we valued the teacher's perspective, we developed a "Who in the Class?" questionnaire which we administered to the teacher. Her responses helped us to further identify (and corroborate our impressions of) children with different styles (Lundsteen, 1983).

Interviews. Interviews, involve the posing of questions to individuals. Once a question is asked, researchers have taken an irreversible step. They have left the tool of observation, where the scene parades before them, and moved into another set of tools, where specific information is sought. Interviews may range from informal conversations to formal interviews with prescribed sets of questions in sequence. They may involve questionnaires, formal surveys, tasks, or projective techniques (which an ethnographer may not use in a standard way). A key informant may be interviewed in depth or several peripheral figures may be asked a few casual, but pertinent, questions. Information may be sought about an event or a life history.

There is a delicate balance between the roles of participant and observer. Not asking questions may result in missing out on important information; on the other hand, being too intrusive may result in the researcher directing the course of events too much. This intrusion may mean that the researcher is not observing an "intact scene" with a naturally developing course of events, but a set of circumstances he has unwittingly helped to create. A safeguard for this type of potential problem is to observe first, getting to know the setting and its people rather well. As ideas begin to occur from the observations, tools of the genre labeled "interview" may be developed or modified in the field.

Written sources. Another set of tools may be classified as "written sources." These might include archival documents and records, less formal written documents such as journals, papers, and stories written by gifted students, or written evidence of library books being checked in and out.

Unwritten records. Unwritten records may include maps, environmental-change diagrams, sociometry diagrams, photographs, films, video and audio tapes, and children's art work. For example, we collected three-dimensional collages made from paper circles that kindergarten children in one study had created. Both their observed behavior in fashioning them and the features of their final product appeared highly informative to us. We "read" information about creative styles and less creative styles into what we collected. These data were confirmed by yet other tasks and observations. When we made maps of the room and school, we could plot how the participants moved through this space, or didn't move, indicating more "style" information.

The following is a sample case of research using multiple tools ("triangulation"). In a recent study (Speck, 1984), the researcher attempted to examine how committed young gifted children were to some creative projects they were working on. She observed the children and included the use of video and audio tapes. She also interviewed the participants (teachers and students) who were involved in these projects. She devised some questionnaires to gain further information. She examined the products of their creative work. Examples were a videotape adaptation of Shakespeare's *A Midsummer Night's Dream*, plays, fiction and non-fiction books, and models. Observation was extensive, examining many long-term projects worked on over a mean period of eight months.

Extended Time Span

Besides theory and multiple tools for fieldwork, another demand of the ethnographic perspective is an extended time span. This kind of research needs large blocks of time in a setting, permitting observation of a full cycle of events. Observation is prolonged and repetitive, e.g., a school year. Furthermore, the researcher needs to allow as much time for analysis and interpretation as for observation. One rule of thumb is: for each day of observation, a day of writing and digestion.

The Researcher as the Research Instrument

Another demand is that the well-trained ethnographer serves as research instrument. And what better tool is there for studying human behavior, in spite of human flaws, than another human being? We might draw an analogy to a human zoom lens, operating alternatively between figure and ground, ground and figure (or part-whole or whole-part). Needed training for these researchers may include not only background knowledge on the topic (e.g., our concern—gifted education) but also how to get information, how to "get along," and the ethics of the interaction (Sieber, 1982). Training may include tasks of noting *key incidents;* frequently these are recurrent events. In addition, key incidents may be examined in relation to other key incidents, to wider social contexts, and to a theoretical base.

Ethnographic Research Cycle

By now it will be evident that the inquiry process demands a research cycle, feeding back on itself. The cycle may include such steps as the following:

1. Select a project while keeping an open mind. (An example might be qualitative assessment of a gifted program for grade three.)

2. Gain access and build rapport. (Start building a relationship of mutual confidence and respect with the administrators, teachers, and students.)

3. Ask questions from an ethnographic perspective. ("What's going on here?") Reformulate questions, making them more specific, as you get into the study and learn more. (For example, "Is the gifted program helping this particular child? Why or why not?" or "What times of day seem to be most productive for this pull-out program?")

4. Collect data in the field. Collect more data as you are informed and revise your questions. (For example, at first watch the whole group at work, as often as possible during the day. Then start observing how one child uses her time. Ask her what she is doing and how she feels about it. Observe the whole group at different specific times to see how the time is used.)

5. Analyze your data and go back for more. (For example, the group came up with more ideas on how to solve a problem on Tuesday than on Wednesday. Why? Sally had a lot to say this week but was almost totally silent during the following week. Was it the change of project?)

These steps are cyclical, not linear. There is an interaction between and among the steps. Questions and constructs are refined at any point, leading to additional data collections using new or changed methods. Hypotheses and questions emerge as the study proceeds in the setting. Guba (1978) envisioned this recurring cycle as an undulating "wave," expanding as one went out to discover, gather data, open one's mind to new possibilities, and then narrowing, as one attempted to verify ideas, gather new data to corroborate, and seeks more specific kinds of information.

A FINAL PRODUCT

The final report gives a description of *what is going on and how it makes sense to those involved.* The final product abstracts the social/cultural patterns (regularities) that serve as a basis for interpreting the descriptions.

Several patterns of social interaction among gifted children were abstracted in a study by Lutz and Lutz (1981). The researchers noticed greater voluntary social interaction among the gifted students during the time they were attending the pull-out program. While with their usual classmates, however, they tended to prefer children not in the gifted program, but who were nevertheless bright. Did the gifted children in this study like having a best friend who was a little less gifted than they because they enjoyed the lack of competition in such a relationship? Is this a general pattern among gifted students? These hypotheses obviously need further testing. Finally, worthy ethnographic study produces a description so that others *can see the generic in the particular.*

In essence, the final product has some predictive power within and across cases regarding behavior. By considering the gifted education classroom as a social system with its own culture, we can expand our perception of gifted education.

Macro and Micro Approaches

Both the procedure and the product may be relatively *macro* or *micro* oriented. *Macro* means a broad, holistic understanding of overall, historical, cultural, or social contexts of a gifted education program. *Micro* may mean the topic is narrowed considerably. In addition, fewer behaviors may be examined.

For example, Janesick (1978) produced a *macro* analysis about what happened when a teacher, who thought he had developed a climate of mutual respect and cooperation in his sixth-grade class, had to get a part-time substitute for six weeks, how the class fell apart, and how he rebuilt the group upon returning. From this macro study Janesick abstracted the teacher's theory of teaching and related it to other theories.

In contrast, a study which is micro oriented might focus on evidence of the type of descriptors, style, world view, and audience orientation that gifted children use in their story-telling. Qualitative analysis may involve thorough, fine-grained examinations of transcripts from audio or video tapes.

Focus

The focus of the final product may be on one or more of five aspects:

1. on the *whole* (culture as an integrative whole).

2. on the *meaning* from the participant's point of view (e.g., what did events mean to Lutz's gifted students and teachers?).

3. on *behavior* (what people did, the forms and functions of behaviors across groups).

4. on the *topic* (the central theme, such as gifted education or creative problem solving).

5. on *hypotheses generation* (hypotheses about events, usually within a general theoretical framework).

6. on *theory.*

An example of the latter is Janesick's (1978) use of theory of symbolic interaction involving interpretive processes, decision making and construction of "self" through actions. Janesick's observed teacher decided that the first priority in teaching was establishing and maintaining a climate of cooperation and mutual respect.

CONCLUSION

The processes used in ethnographic research and the products which emanate from it are not unnatural to us. Most of us are used to observing behavior in our gifted programs—looking at unique detail, noting shared characteristics in common with other instances, events, or cases. We try to get an overall "feel" for what is going on. We ask, as would an ethnographer, "Of what, is this case of a gifted child, representative?"

The methods which are used in assessing from an ethnographic perspective have rigor yet flexibility. Within a broad cultural context, this ethnographic perspective "watches and asks," with ample time to find out. Admittedly a human instrument can be faulted as too detached and too involved, too subject to bias and to illness—and yet still be the most sensitive instrument we have come upon.

Advantages of qualitative methods are that they help us to better understand the central processes in which teachers and gifted children are engaged. These methods can give us depth of understanding, and fruitful hypotheses to test. They can uncover patterns of gifted children's responses and help us avoid the error of oversimplifying. They can provide triangulation, thorough field work, and disciplined notions from ethnography. Classes of events may be better understood through thorough examination of particular cases.

With respect to productive education of the gifted, qualitative research may be our least used way of assessing programs. Yet, it may be the most promising way of knowing "where we are going, how we will get there, and how we will know we've arrived."

In conclusion, it may be helpful to suggest some sample research questions.

Some Questions for Ethnographic Research with the Gifted

1. What are the social roles gifted children play during their education?

2. What rules do they construct and follow in their social interaction?

3. How do participants in gifted programs hold one another accountable in relationship to tasks?

4. What are the varieties of processes and materials available for gifted students to choose from? How are these interacting with gifted abilities and education?

5. What are social interactional consequences of varying innovations in gifted education? (For example, consider competitive, cooperative, and cooperative and individual activities.)

6. In what contexts do gifted abilities flourish?

7. What other cases and contexts support, contradict, or expand present findings?

In general—"What's going on here?"

REFERENCES

Bogdan, R. C., & Biklen, S. K. (1982). *Qualitative research for education.* Boston: Allyn & Bacon.

Goodenough, W. (1971). *Culture, language and society.* Reading, MA: Addison-Wesley.

Guba, E. G. (1978). *Toward a methodology of naturalistic inquiry in educational evaluation.* Los Angeles: University of California, Center for the Study of Evaluation.

Heath, S. B. (1982). Ethnography in education: Defining the essentials. In P. Gilmore & A. Glatthorn (Eds.), *Children in and out of schools.* Washington, DC: Center for Applied Linguistics.

Janesick, V. J. (1978). An ethnographic study of a teacher's classroom perspective: Implications for curriculum. *Monographs of the Institute for Research on Teaching, 33.* East Lansing: Michigan State University.

Lundsteen, S. W. (1983). Problem solving of Swedish and American children. *National Council of Teachers of English.* NCTE International Assembly, 14–19. (Newsletter, yearly edition).

Lutz, F. W., & Lutz, S. B. (1981). Gifted pupils in the elementary school setting. *The Creative Child and Adult Quarterly, 4*(2), 93–102.

Mager, R. F. (1968). *Developing attitude toward learning.* Belmont, CA: Fearon.

Sieber, J. E. (1982). *The ethics of social research.* New York: Springer-Verlag.

Speck, A. M. (1984). *The task commitment of young gifted children: A micro-ethnographic study of the effects of teacher and peer behavior on creative productivity.* Unpublished doctural dissertation, University of Connecticut.

Story, C. M. (1985). Facilitator of learning: A micro-ethnographic study of the teacher of the gifted. *Gifted Child Quarterly, 29,* 155–159.

Wolcott, H. (1980). Ethnographic research in education. In R. M. Jaegar (Ed.), *Alternative methodologies in educational research* (AERA Cassette Tape Series L-2). Washington, DC: AERA Central Office.

Index

Note: References to tables or figures are indicated by *italic type* and the addition of *"t"* or *"f"* respectively.

**CORWIN
PRESS**

The Corwin Press logo—a raven striding across an open book—represents the union of courage and learning. Corwin Press is committed to improving education for all learners by publishing books and other professional development resources for those serving the field of K–12 education. By providing practical, hands-on materials, Corwin Press continues to carry out the promise of its motto: **"Helping Educators Do Their Work Better."**